A Mountain Monday

Bruce Sloan

Parson's Porch Books

A Mountain Monday
ISBN: Softcover 978-1-960326-43-0
Copyright © 2023 by Bruce Sloan

Parson's Porch Books is an imprint of Parson's Porch *&* Company (PP*&*C) in Cleveland, Tennessee. PP*&*C is a self-funded charity which earns money by publishing books of noted authors, representing all genres. Its face and voice is **David Russell Tullock** who you can contact at: dtullock@parsonsporch.com.

Parson's Porch *&* Company *turns books into bread & milk* by sharing its profits with the poor.

www.parsonsporch.com

A Mountain Monday

Contents

Introduction

The early American landscape painters would often paint, in the background of their art, magnificent towering mountains. These beautiful mountains represented the power and majesty of God. Whatever the landscape, we are drawn to the great hope and protection found in God the Creator.

Mountains have also been seen as having a special place to the understanding of the spiritual life. Both Moses and Jesus had important events on the mountain. "And the LORD said unto Moses, Come up to me into the mount, and be there: and I will give thee tables of stone, and a law, and commandments which I have written; that thou may teach them." (Exodus 24:12) "And after he (Jesus) had taken leave of them, he went up on the mountain to pray. Immediately before choosing his twelve apostles." (Mark 6:46)

In Japan, Mount Fuji is very much understood as a spiritual mountain for the Japanese. Mount Taylor in New Mexico is seen as a sacred mountain to the Navajo Nation. In almost every nation, there are mountains that call for the spiritual part of our life to lift our eyes unto the hills. Some take pilgrimages up the mountain. There is a sense of being closer to God, not so much in physical distance but in spiritual awareness.

Mondays are the beginning of the week for secular life. Saturday and Sundays are marked as days of rest and worship. As some say, "we live for the weekends." And that leaves Monday as the culprit of ending our happy time. We are called back to our work, our labor, our schedules set by others. There is this feeling of beginning all over to make it to Friday.

And yet, Monday is a day that God has given to us. It is a day that all of God's promises hold true for us. The word Monday came from an earlier English word for Moon. The Moon is essential for the immigration of birds and the impact of the ocean tides. It is the work of our Mondays to guide us into a new week. Just as our spiritual life is to guide us, so are the Mondays that we face. It really becomes an opportunity to adjust our secular understanding of Monday to a spiritual awareness that every day is a good day in God's realm.

Mountain Monday is a simple way to express that God has made both the mountains and our Mondays for His glory and our good. It is just how we want to make the day. On a mountain or not, we are God's greatest love.

Bruce Sloan

A Spiritual Life

"May the God of peace himself sanctify you entirely; and may your spirit and soul and body be kept sound and blameless at the coming of our Lord Jesus Christ." 1 Thessalonians 5:23

In the early days of my education, it seemed to me that the school officials attempted to make Friday a day to dread. It was the day for fried government fish, spelling tests, and open assembly. And then on the way out of class for home, the teacher reminded us "Be sure to do your homework. There will be a test on Monday." Now one of the great things about being an adult is that there are no tests on Friday.

Perhaps I would have been a better student if I had studied for the test. I studied the material that I liked. The teacher's mind and my mind never seemed to be on the same wave link. My understanding of poems and literature seldom matched the wisdom of the teacher. Geometry seemed to be a lottery of finding which law went with each angle. The teacher expressed how geometry would help us organize our life. Perhaps, this is one reason my study is in such a mess.

I love to learn, and along the way I had some wonderful and precious teachers. They must have made an impression, because studying is probably my hobby. And it serves me well as a pastor in preparing several lessons a week. I still find it exciting to open the Bible and begin to see what God has waiting for me. Reading, research and theological discussion makes a good day for me.

One of the challenges as a pastor is to relate how all that we are learning, or doing, or thinking about, can relate to the spiritual life. Matthew Fox wrote that in America we are so divided within our own life by separating everything. We are almost in conflict within ourselves. We see our work, our play, our faith as distinct activities. We do not see them as one in the development of our spiritual life. Our spirit, soul and body appear to be working on different levels.

To be a whole person spiritually is to see all that we encounter as a part of our spiritual progress. We participate in building oneness or wholeness in many respects as we live. We mix ingredients to make a meal, we drive a car that is made of many parts, and we exercise to stay in shape. But the exercise also is a way to enhance our spiritual being. We struggle with the spiritual a lot because we fail to see how important all that we do is essentially spiritual.

Enjoying the fog lift off of the mountain, struggling to find an item at the grocery store, or listening to YouTube is a part of our spiritual life. God created us as one. Our Spirit, Soul and Body works as one. And when we accept that, we will find a great peace in our lives.

Obey

Therefore go and make disciples of all nations, baptizing them in the name of the Father and of the Son and of the Holy Spirit, and teaching them to obey everything I have commanded you. And surely I am with you always, to the very end of the age. Matthew 28:19-20

Every genuine Baptist knows the scripture by heart. It is the call to action and service. It is the scripture that has sent millions of Christian missionaries into the world to share the Good News of Jesus Christ. Can you imagine a world without Jesus?

I say the word "genuine" because there are some people who just drove by a Baptist Church all of their lives, but never went in. Normally in their obituary it is written, "they were of the Baptist faith." I do not want to be critical, but the door to Heaven is not under a Baptist sign.

There is one thing that many Baptists agree on, and they do not agree on a lot. As you have probably noticed, there are a lot of Baptist churches around. And if you go into those churches you will see a large aisle dividing the pews. We say about the divisions, "They kept the furniture, but we kept the faith." But what most Baptists believe is that you have to go down into the water to be baptized. It is symbolic for us. We have died unto Jesus and now have been resurrected into a new life to live forever with Christ.

Having friends in many Christian denominations, I take some kidding about our form of baptism. It is important to us, but normally I say: "We Baptists have more sins to wash out than most." I have witnessed baptisms all over the world with the same result. Joyful people coming up out of the water with a new hope for life. This is indeed good news.

In most parts of the world, baptisms are done outside. There are rivers, lakes and oceans that provide a beautiful scene as people walk down to the water's edge. Beckoned by the preacher, they go into the water to answer in obedience to the call of Jesus in their life. In the United States, we prefer the warm waters of an indoor baptistry. We like to have it our way. Believe me, warm or cold water, the life of a Christian is not a call to live on an easy street. It is the first step of a dangerous journey, but with the hand of an ever-faithful God to watch over us to the end.

Now, the part about teaching people to obey is another matter. It is like trying to teach my cat, Tango, to obey. She looks at me and decides if she wants to do something or not. I get that same look from some Baptists when I talk to them about obeying Christ. If some of my Baptist brethren would stop being so naughty, thinking that they are the Word, and just obey God's true Word, we would have a wonderful day in the neighborhood. "Trust and obey" was in our old Baptist hymnal. Maybe we need to dust that old song off and sing it.

Promises

"Just say a simple, 'Yes, I will,' or 'No, I won't. Anything beyond this is from the evil one" Matthew 5:37

It was a simple time of playing with my five-year-old granddaughter when she asked me if I would take her to Paris. Angela and I had been telling the grandchildren about our travels, and the trip to Paris was shared. It sounded like such a wonderful place to a child that she wanted to go. So, she asked me, "Papa, will you take me to Paris?"

And as all good grandparents do when the grandchildren are around, I said: "Of course I will. When you grow up, I will take you to Paris." Now, years later, the question comes to me, "Papa, I am so looking forward to our trip to Paris."
I asked Angela, "When did I say I would take her to Paris?"

Young minds are a wonderful thing, especially when they remember what you have promised years later. I do not think a Philadelphia lawyer can get me out of this one. We do make promises. Sometimes they are well thought out and at other times we rush to a promise that is going to be difficult. We make many promises through life. Some of them to ourselves, or to our family and even to God. The intention is good, but the cost is often lost in the consideration.

Such as when we became a Christian. We made a covenant or promise to God that we would make Jesus Christ our Lord and Savior. We said by our public testimony of baptism that now we would forever follow Christ. It is a promise that does come with a price. "I have been crucified with Christ; and it is no longer I that live, but Christ liveth in me: and that life which I now live in the flesh I live in faith, the faith, which is in the Son of God, who loved me, and gave himself up for me." (Galatians 2:20

A lot of promises are made in our lives. Thoughtful promises of following Christ, or keeping an oath of office, or to a marriage partner. And then those promises made without giving much thought, such as a promised trip to Paris to a child. The Bible says we are to let our word be true. If we say yes then yes or no then no. There is always a cost to a promise.

Paris? Really, Paris? I wonder if going to Paris, Tennessee will count? If not, I hope the loan officer at the bank gets out on the happy side of his bed in the morning.

The Weather

Fire and hail, snow and clouds; Stormy wind, fulfilling His word; Psalm 148:8

In the South, we often begin our conversations about the weather. We have a weather channel, weather alerts on our phones, and a very nice umbrella in the closet as we rush to the car in a rainstorm. Of course, the weather person said it was going to rain.

Weather can even give you a hint of a person's political stand. One must walk lightly around the question, "You don't believe in all of this climate change? Do you?" Well, yes I do. Weather has always changed. In the third grade, I remember the local radio station having a program about weather. It was a belief back in the 1950s that one day Michigan would have warm beaches and Florida would be a frozen glacier. How is that for local prophecy? It did not convince me to move north.

The Bible has numerous scriptures on the weather. We remember Jonah who really should have listened to the weather report. In the deserts of Abraham, Moses and Jesus, there was a need for rain. Not only for rain, but rain that came in the right season. Three rains are often mentioned. Without all three the crops would not make it. Thank goodness for Joseph who unwittingly went ahead to Egypt so his people could survive the drought.

The issue might be if we believe or do not believe that we mere humans can make the weather change. Is it possible that the ever-increasing population of the world, the paving of every trail in the forest and more cows than ever giving off gas in the fields has any effect on the environment? The environment that we create does make a difference in our health.

There is a thought in the Bible that at the end of time there will be a massive explosion on the earth that will transform all creation into darkness. Those who worry about nuclear warheads believe this is a distinct possibility. And then there just might be a little boy sitting out in a grass field with a lot of cows who lights up his rabbit tobacco cigar that ignites the whole world on fire.

But be assured, this will not happen until God decides it is time. Until then as the Psalmist says, "Let them praise the name of the Lord, for his name alone is exalted." And be very kind to God's gift to us, the earth and all that dwells there in. We are responsible.

A Crutch to Share

Two are better than one; because they have a good reward for their labour. For if they fall, the one will lift up his fellow: but woe to him that is alone when he falleth; for he hath not another to help him up. Again, if two lie together, then they have heat: but how can one be warm alone? And if one prevail against him, two shall withstand him; and a threefold cord is not quickly broken. Ecclesiastes 4:9-12

For two weeks, Angela and I joined our son and his family for a trip to Cuba. Angela's family has had a connection to the Baptist work there for over a hundred years. I have only been once before with a choir festival. Jonathan said he would plan the trip if we would come along. It was a wonderful trip.

The country is open to visit if one goes to "help the Cuban people." Delta Airlines and American Airlines fly there several times a week. This was the first time we were on our own to see the country and to experience the wonderful Cubans. Our grandchildren loved it. And by the way, it is a very safe place to go.

It is a land of a photographer's delight. Everywhere you look there is an award-winning photo. Sugar cane fields, horse drawn carriages and an extravagant number of Colonial buildings, and yes, there are those old 1950's and 60's automobiles. And for the farmer, there are tractors that go back to the Garden of Eden.

My favorite photo was taken toward the end of the trip. I was walking down a street in Havana when I saw a couple walking in front of me. They were old and frail. The were holding hands and one was using a metal crutch. After a moment, I saw him hand it to his wife so she could use it some. There in the midst of the city was a couple sharing an old crutch.

Perhaps a book could be written about their life. The struggles through revolutions, economic down turns, doing without, but still together holding hands. They did not have enough money for two sets of crutches, but one old crutch served them well enough. And we think we need so much in our lives to be happy.

I saw young kids with no toys drawing cars on the streets to ride in; small windows from a home filled with fruits and vegetables to sell; a man finishing a wall with concrete celebrating his new art work. "Come" he said, "take a photo." And I did.

My passport visa said I was in Cuba to help the people. But sometimes we are helped more by the vision of sharing, joy in a piece of chalk or on a 105-degree summer day renewing a wall of concrete.

The Future

"Trust in the Lord forever, for the Lord is a rock for all ages."
Isaiah 26:4

There was a very practical reason for God wanting us to increase our faith. The Creator knew that one day we would be riding in our grandchild's car. It was not enough to ride with your child as they first approached the interstate entrance ramp. As it has often been said; "Don't cry when the children leave home, they will be back with more kids." And as grandparents, we love and enjoy each one. It is difficult to sit on the other side of the driver and watch that kid maneuver the car. Not so much about the danger, but about life quickly passing.

A lot has passed since I learned to drive the old Dodge Ram car with the exciting A.M. radio blaring the morning farm report. Windows were down, and the steering wheel seemed to be three feet across. With a good strong steel dashboard there would be no need for seat belts. And our parents did not seem to be very concerned about our future. We were just to "go off and make them proud."

Today, I hear a lot of talk about how "we are concerned for the future, and especially the grandchildren." Some of the fear relates to the new world of electronics, cultural unrest, and an environment that is straining our water supply. Employment, healthcare, and the "attitude" of the coming generation clouds our vision of the future. It is like the mountain mist that slowly engulfs you as you drive along the mountain road.

I believe the future will be okay for the kids. The reason is that I believe in God. And I believe God keeps all of His promises. The next generations are not going to do it our way. They will remember us sitting in the car when they first drove up on the interstate. They will remember reading the Bible and praying with us. They might even remember some of our childhood stories. The important thing is that they remember us for having faith in them for the future.

Our speech for the future is not of fear but of faith. We do not worry for tomorrow because God has called us to trust in Him always. The Psalmist said: "Be still and know that I am God. I will be exalted among the nations; I will be exalted in the earth!" (Psalm 46:10) God is not frightened for the future. All generations adapt to their time of life, just as you and I have. Maybe we are fearful because we do not have faith in our future.

Let us speak of faith, hope, joy and love. It is not just for Christmas time. It is also for the future.

Artificial Intelligence

"The earth is the Lord's and all it holds"
Psalm 24:1

I was asked if I believed AI (Artificial Intelligence) would take over the world. There is always a temptation to give a humorous answer in return. Yet, I believe the sincere question deserves a sincere answer. Without a mini sermon the answer is "No." As mere humans, we have always been a little frightened about our species surviving. It has not kept us from creating weapons of mass destruction or filling the ocean with plastic or drugging ourselves silly.

My only hope in all things is God. As one Christian confession of faith states, "our whole purpose is to glorify God." I believe most religious groups have a similar statement of belief. We were made in the image of God to bring joy to the Creator. Of course, through time we have modified that to mean our purpose is to glorify ourselves. God has not created us to destroy us. God has made you and me for Himself.

Throughout our history, we have been nervous when new things were created around us. I imagine when the first fire was started the woman told the man, "you have gone and done it now." Every so many years a new invention brings both joy and concern. The wheel, the boat, the airplane, the computer, all were suspect. But by in large, these inventions have made our lives better. Do you remember when we were told that with the computer we would no longer need paper? Now we purchase paper by the box rather than by a small packet.

I think we are all surprised by how quickly our internet devices receive offers to purchase something that we had recently looked up on our phone or computer. I am still getting offers for a concrete mixer for a job I did several years ago. This is the world of "marketing." This keeps the poor poor and the rich rich. The World of Coca-Cola was the first to master the art.

The greater concern might be the possibility that artificial intelligence could replace our own thinking. Perhaps we might become the servant of the robot. Actually, we probably do not give much time to our own thinking. We just absorb all of the news and views around us. God calls on us to meditate on The Word, and those good things that have come our way. Thinking is good.

So we might just take a moment to see if we have already given into AI providing our life's answers rather than seeking God to glorify Him. As in all new things, AI will do a lot of good and also cause some harm if we let it. But "no" God is going to keep us around until "that day."

Memorial Day

Remember the day you stood before the Lord your God at Horeb, when the Lord said to me, 'Assemble the people to Me, that I may let them hear My words so they may learn to fear Me all the days they live on the earth, and that they may teach their children. Deuteronomy 4:10

B efore the People of God entered the promised land, Moses gave some rules and laws that should be carefully followed. It is like the time your parents gave you a list of do's and don'ts before you drove off in the family car. This is going to be a new and exciting experience, but there are some directions to keep this a good and productive time for you.

Now, as we get older, we get into the car (once I would say jump into the car) and seldom think of all of the lectures we received about safe driving. We just assume we are a good driver and enjoy the trip. The next major lecture on driving will be from our kids when they look as if they are going to take the keys away. And as all intelligent adults, we have a hidden set.

Yet memory is important. We do need to remember that God has set this wonderful world up with some essential truths that will guide us to a full and beneficial life. There seems to be a lot of rules in the Bible. When taken one at a time they are helpful and will keep us out of a lot of trouble.

Today in the United States we are called to "remember" those who gave their lives in the battles of our nation. They did not create the wars, but they came forward when the trumpet sounded. Their lives and their families deserved to be remembered. In church, before we said the pledge to the American flag, the leader spoke the names of his military roommates, flight instructors and friends who died in the Vietnam War. It was an honor to hear those names in our sanctuary....young men remembered for their ultimate sacrifice.

I live close to a national military cemetery. On occasion, I have funerals to attend. It is a place that is marked with hillside after hillside of those who gave something more than words to this nation. They gave their lives. The flag that is above them today is not just colors, it was a call that came. They met it with all that they had. Yes, we need to remember.

We need to also remember that God has high expectations of us. Kathrine Bates wrote, "Till all success be nobleness and every gain divine." (America the Beautiful). Yes, yes, yes may we see our future as noble people who have accomplished what our God desires. That will be a wonderful result of the memory of those who gave all to our nation.

Baptists

*Remember ye not the former things, neither consider the things
of old. Behold, I will do a new thing; now it shall spring forth;
shall ye not know it? I will even make a way in the wilderness,
and rivers in the desert.* Isaiah 43:18-19

The Southern Baptist Convention was formed in 1845.
Many of the churches that formed the new convention
had been a part of the Triennial Convention. The Southern
Baptist Convention was formed because the Triennial
Convention would not approve slave-holding missionaries.
Many of the founders of the new convention owned slaves.
Not in a real hurry to do so, it was in 1995 that the convention
apologized for its stance on slavery. Well, we did vote on a
resolution. The convention resolutions have little or no impact
on the local congregation.

In 1914, a Texas Baptist hymnal publisher R.H. Coleman,
announced a vote for the next year to allow women to attend
as messengers. A messenger is a person elected by the local
church to attend the annual meeting. It caused a lot of agony
since women could not even vote in political elections at that
time. Eventually, in 1918 the vote was taken to allow women
to vote at the convention. The "Women's Issue" continues
until today.

The convention met in New Orleans to talk about "the
women." A city that has worked very hard to portray women
in a negative way. There appears to be a group of Baptists that
believe women should not be allowed near the pulpit. Perhaps
if they were going to sweep around or polish it they could
approach the diadem. The formal dress today at the pulpit is

tennis shoes, blue jeans, and holding a microphone. Freud would have a holiday talking about that sight.

Albert Camus, an atheist, was invited to speak to a group of Christians. He said that if Christians would speak out clearly against the evils of the day that the churches would be filled. But when a pastor prays before a group about to do evil then the Christian witness is lost. Sometimes those who are on the other side know more than we do about who we really are.

R. H. Tawney wrote "Most generations walk in a path which they neither make nor discover but accept. The main thing is that they must march." And it is against this accepting unacceptable behavior that the Christian should stand. Isaiah said: "I will even make a way in the wilderness, and rivers in the desert." We should be leading the way to the wholeness of every creature of God. We are the ones called to tell the Good News of God's redemption and reclaiming the dignity of all.

Voting to restrict a person from the pulpit and then walking down Bourbon street is not the Christian witness we should give.

Saints

"Greet every saint in Christ Jesus.
The brothers who are with me greet you.
All the saints greet you,
especially those of Caesar's household"
Philippians 4:21-22

In the final note of a letter to Philippi, Paul makes a remarkable statement of greetings: " ... especially those of Caesar's household." Indeed Caesar was the most powerful man in the world at this moment. He held his hand tightly around his kingdom. There would be little that he would not notice, especially in his own house. The city of Philippi was a major trading post for the Romans, and Caesar would be considered god.

Now, in the midst of this house, were Christians. Paul refers to them as saints. All religions have a special word designated for "saint," but the word saint is a word unique to the Christian community. A saint is often thought of as a holy person who has died. However, it is also used to express the "holiness" or "saintliness" of a living Christian.

Paul paid a particular phrase of honor to those Christians who were in a challenging and difficult situation. They could immediately be put to death and their families killed. They were brave in their faithfulness in seeing Yahweh as the only God through Jesus Christ. The church itself in the city was very small. They could only count on the protection of God.

This scripture points us to a reality of one's faith. We live out our faith not because it is popular, or politically powerful, or of great profit for us. We live out our faith because it is a "peace that passes all understanding," "a living hope of a resurrection that is imperishable," and "a joy unspeakable." As Paul said, "For in Christ we live, and move, and have our being." Whatever environment God has placed us in, we are confident He is able to keep us to the end.

Often, we remark about how things are changing around us. Indeed, we have seen many changes. Our children and grandchildren will see more changes. Christianity will endure much, but the very foundation of our faith is that God will never leave us. I have never lived in an environment of Caesar's household. But I know many do. For them I pray, and I give thanks for the place God has given me.

Ethics

"Speak to the entire assembly of Israel and say to them:
Be holy because I, the LORD your God, am holy.
Leviticus 19:2

A P. Sorokin wrote in his book *Altruistic Love*, "There are times when mankind needs an upsurge of scientific discoveries. And at times there is a paramount need for the release of religious creativity. Finally, there are periods when the greatest need is ethical living at its noblest, wisest and best." He went on to say that this is the time we need ethical living.

Almost every profession has a requirement for ethical instruction. And yet we see such poor ethics on a daily basis. In the Christian community, we hide behind our religion, others hide behind a constitution. There is a long journey to take in building a national ethical character.

The tragic murders tallying higher each day, denying women equality and watching the homeless piled into large dumps speaks of a need of some serious change. And as a Baptist, I do know we do not like change. Yet, someone needs to say that we are not even telling ourselves the truth.

"Prayers and thoughts" have become a camouflage for serious Christian living. "Prayers and thoughts" is not a magical formula where we say words and suddenly everything is fine. I pray a lot, and I am greatly comforted by knowing God hears me. But I am also aware that prayer is not a one-sided conversation. A greater part of prayer is "listening." Prayer is not static. It is not a command for God to a make everything the way I want it. Prayer is a Holy charge to be honest with God and with myself. Prayer moves me to action. It might be to forgive, to visit, to write, and even to change. Prayer is faith that God can do all things. And often God begins with me.

In the early political organizing of America, there was a sincere belief that this new nation would become one out of many different nations. There was also a belief that there would be some kind of "inner check" where all of the people would live in peace. The idea for the phrase, "One Nation Under God" came from this thought. But this "inner check" never came to be. We place it on our most valuable money and it has not worked.

For those of faith, we must return to the God that made us. We must become Holy as our God is Holy, not in our own ability or wisdom, but in the salvation that Jesus presents to us. It will not be us who change the world, it will be God who works through us.

So, let us come out and live Holy lives for the glory of God.

Old Churches

And I say also unto thee, That thou art Peter, and upon this rock I will build my church; and the gates of hell shall not prevail against it. Matthew 16:18

My wife and I took a trip to Europe where we enjoyed studying the churches and music. It came at a good time for me when so many are discouraged by the church attendance in our own nation. The old traditional churches are struggling as a few of the more modern churches seem to be holding on. As a pastor of the traditional church, I also wonder about the state of the church in the United States.

Taking advantage of my wife's good nature, we visited a number of old churches and cathedrals. All of the places we visited are still active congregations. The buildings go back over a thousand years. They have had to rebuild after devastating wars and plagues. Our churches in America are young babes compared to the history of European churches. Somehow, these old European buildings continue to be filled with the hymns of praise and the preached Word. The congregations are not large, but they are faithful and steadfast.

As the Apostle Paul said, we see with a dim eye the future. Our future is tomorrow. For God, the future is eternal. I have in my office a painting of a church in Scotland. It is a church where one of my ancestors pastored in the 15th century. Often, I look at the painting and see the promise that God never gives up on His church. Half of the church building appears in ruins and half has been rebuilt for current worship. The buildings are not the church, but they are evidence that there have been people who worshiped God.

The old Gospel song, "I don't know about tomorrow, but I know who holds my hand" is a good theme for our future. We will continue to build and rebuild buildings, but God continues to build the church that "the gates of hell shall not prevail against it." The church has never had it easy. In America, we have enjoyed a number of "easy" years of church building. But that is not the norm for church history. We walk a narrow path that is always lit by the presence of God. Darkness, storms and enemies all around, but the Savior has promised never to leave us or forsake us.

And these are the years God has chosen for us to live out our faith. Let us hold strong and keep our eye on the Cross. It is our hope and eternal future.

Sin

He was oppressed, and he was afflicted, yet he opened not his mouth: he is brought as a lamb to the slaughter, and as a sheep before her shearers is dumb, so he openeth not his mouth.
Isaiah 53:7

For several months I worked at updating our home shower. A part of the process was replacing the shower walls with ceramic tiles. It takes forever, but I enjoy the process of creating a wall of small tiles. I am not a master tile setter, but a master of thinking that I am. Up and down the stairs I go down to the garage to cut the tiles. I then return down the stairs to cut them some more. My wife has given me so many measuring tapes that I have lost count. Practicing the "hit and miss" method is one of my skills.

On one of my journeys up and down the stairs, I tripped. This is a real big "no, no" when you reach my age. The tile flew out of my hands across the floor as I landed face down. My wife comes over to check if I were injured. Thankfully, I was fine. Then she looked at the bottom of one of my shoes with the rubber sole almost detached.

"How long have you been wearing these old shoes with floppy soles?" she asked. She takes the shoes and says, "These are going into the trash right now." And so goes my favorite pair of shoes. They have carried me many miles in many countries. They were like my partner in places I wanted to go. And now, in a moment, they are gone. Like many, I have good shoes, but only one pair of special shoes that I always wear. The Pope even did not say anything about their shape when I visited the Vatican a few years ago.

Jesus "opened not his mouth." There are a lot of profound things he could have said. He could have pointed out every sin in everyone's life standing around them. He could have caused a political storm, or even called for an earthquake. Yet, in his precious holy way, Jesus stood calm. He knew that one day a fellow by the name of Bruce would need his sins forgiven.

What sins? Some of those things we think or do have no place in the life of one who seeks God. We call them, "Our favorite little sins." They do not bother other people, and they do not bother us. But then one day, when least expected, that little "loose" sin causes us to tumble. "Why?" we ask when confronted with the consequence of such a small sin.

Jesus is a part of the creation to give us a new perspective of a good life. Everyone in that room with Jesus had their own idea of what was right and what was wrong. But they did not see the real answer looking right back at them. Sometimes, we become so arrogant with our own way that we do not see the right way. And Jesus waits silently for us even today for our response.

Easter Sacrifice

Jesus said to her (Martha), "I am the resurrection and the life. The one who believes in me will live, even though they die."
John 11:25

In the early days of my spiritual journey, Jesus did not need gymnasiums or smoking rooms or extremely large televisions screens. It seemed all that Jesus needed at that time was an open mind and an open heart. Faith was not so much about me, but about a God who loved me.

The Easter season is here. Well, for a lot of Christians it started a few weeks back at Ash Wednesday. Actually, the day after the wild party in New Orleans called Mardi Gras (French for Fat Tuesday) that seems to define our secular enjoyment of a very tragic spiritual event. The Easter season moves through a time of seeking forgiveness of our sins. And as in all things Christian, Easter is celebrated on different days by different Christian groups.

Baptists have somewhat remained aloof from these days of Lent, Holy Week, and the beautiful worship of Orthodox Christians that end at sunrise of Easter Day. We have chosen a simpler lifestyle of a nice Easter dress, family over for lunch and maybe some white lilies. We do not have the crucifixion cross in our houses of worship or a burning Easter Candle. Our theology is that of the Resurrection. He Lives and should live in our hearts.

The Baptist theologian, W. A. Carver, wrote a book about the <u>Self Interpretation of Jesus</u> (1936). He tells us that a large part of the Gospels relate to the last few days of Christ. The

35

importance of this event is paramount in understanding the meaning of the life, death and resurrection of Christ. So often we spend a lot of time with the general life of Christ and its interpretation today. However, the writers of the Gospel focused on the final moments of God's only Son.

It makes me think that as much as we are a "resurrection" people, we are also a people indebted to the pain and suffering of the Son of God. Whatever grief there has been in our life, none compares to the grief of God who presents His only son for our misbehavior and evil ways. Our sin is a big disappointment to God. And even in that disappointment, God loved us so much.

In this day, let us not forget the power of sacrifice made for each of us. Yes, Easter morning is coming, but it comes at a great expense for the only Son of God.

Home Repairs

"For every house is built by someone,
but God is the builder of everything."
Hebrews 3:4

Our family has lived in our current home for sixteen years. We love the location and the house itself. Having traveled to new churches to serve as pastor through the years. We enjoy this place very much. We have lived in some beautiful homes in some wonderful settings, but having your own home is a special blessing to us. Our first home was in the Black Jack community of Decatur County, Georgia. Kids would ride up on their ponies to play with our daughter. The last place we lived was in a one room apartment in Old Town Vilnius Lithuania. We would eat pizza in the open-air cafes in front of our building.

We have been in this home long enough to start making repairs. It is a well-built home, but as all buildings, it needs a constant updating. Wooden floors replaced carpeting, tile being replaced, windows replaced, and the list continues. I love to work around the house as an eager novice carpenter. Now the current fad is to refinish the bathroom with a walk-in-shower. There are companies that can redo a bathroom in one day. I think I can refinish one before the new year comes. Of course, that makes for some interesting comments as the days turn into weeks.

I have the greatest admiration of buildings that have survived under unbelievable conditions. The great stone buildings of Scotland, the ancient yellow clay brick structures of Peru, and the red buildings of Santa Fe. We are even seeing some structures coming back to life as the water recedes in lakes because of the drought, Even with these structures, there has to be a certain amount of repairs.

The Godly life compels us to keep working on our own house of faith. Our very being cries out to be fed with the wondrous Word of God. The hard-working people of the past would take time off once a week to rest. It was a necessity for both body and spirit to be renewed on a regular basis. Sitting in the midst of family and friends singing, praying and listening to a sermon was the highlight of the week. You do not work your mule every day of the week. You give the laborers time to be with their loved ones. Even the fields need to lay at rest for a season.

We do build, but God is building something greater within us. And what God is building within us is eternal. It does take time. The grand architect of our life is careful in every detail. It is not like some of my haphazard hammering of a nail or getting it almost right. God is perfection and when we allow God the use of our life for His work, it will be true and straight.

In our stress of trying to do it all, there is another way. God has a great understanding of who you and I really are. And I believe God's love would like to do a greater work in our life. It is going to take more than a day, but then we do have eternity.

How Long?

How long wilt thou forget me, O Lord? forever? how long wilt thou hide thy face from me? How long shall I take counsel in my soul, having sorrow in my heart daily? How long shall mine enemy be exalted over me? Psalm 13

How Long, O Lord? When we are facing a crisis. This is a question that has been from the foundation of the world. It is the moment that we realize that we are so very dependent on God. We appreciate the scientists who are working to bring healing and longer lives. But sometimes we know science will not be the answer.

The Psalmist continued "Consider and hear me, O Lord my God: lighten mine eyes, lest I sleep the sleep of death." This is a plea by the great king of Israel to spare him the tragedy that he faces. He understands that without the help of God through this time he will not make it. This is a very human and honest request to give him some peace for whatever is ahead. We enter these restless times in our world where even friends have become suspicious of our decisions about so much and so many conspiracy theories.

How Long, O Lord? The Israeli martyr Hannah Szenes wrote:

> To die…so young to die…no, no not I
> I love the warm sunny skies …
> But praise be He for the grace …
> If I should die today

The Psalmist concluded: "But I have trusted in thy mercy; my heart shall rejoice in thy salvation. I will sing unto the Lord, because he hath dealt bountifully with me." In God's timing, our crisis will come to an end. And through it all, we will see our faith and hope grow in the everlasting God. We will weep with those who weep, we will hold the hands of those who need a friend, and we will not judge those who differ with us on this matter.

Seneca wrote: Courage is the scorner of the things which inspire fear.

Jesus said to her (Martha), "I am the resurrection and the life. The one who believes in me will live, even though they die; and whoever lives by believing in me will never die. Do you believe this?"

Glorify God

The heavens declare the glory of God;
and the firmament sheweth his handywork.
Psalm 19:1

We live in an area where the beauty of the heavens and the earth are astonishing. Perhaps where anyone has lived and called home there is a feeling that this must be one of the most beautiful places in the world. And indeed it is, as all of Creation is the work of God.

When we take time to study the creation, we find there is far more than what we first see. Volumes can be written about any part of Creation. E. O. Wilson became a famous biologist by studying the ant as a child. The Creation has a way of drawing us into a new world of the remarkable, if not miraculous.

In observing the heavens, there is a constant movement of color, shapes and sounds. Artists have used the heavens to create paintings, operas and architecture. As the clouds cross the sky we often see animals, flowers or even people's faces in them. Such delight we can find in the heavens declaring their glory to God.

Movement must please God. The Scripture speaks of worship at the temple as being a movement. The church is constantly called to movement. Jesus says that He is building in heaven for us. And God reminds us that the Creator's purpose and will is unfolding every day.

And as all that glorifies God is in movement, we find ourselves somewhat resistant to movement. We often comment on how every time we read the Scriptures we get something new out of them. God challenges us to go observe the ant to see the power of faith at work. And God challenges us to grow deep. The Apostle Paul tells us to:

> *"Let your roots grow down into him, and let your lives be built on him. Then your faith will grow strong in the truth you were taught, and you will overflow with thankfulness."*
> Colossians 2:7

We see the beauty of the Heavens declaring glory to God, We think of how we wish we could create such a lovely painting of the sky above. How do we bring such praise and glory to God? And we, the highest of all creation, are simply asked to glorify God, and to enjoy Him forever. I believe there might need to be a little more movement in our glorifying God.

Relaxing

"The Lord is good to those whose hope is in him, to the one who seeks him; it is good to wait quietly for the salvation of the Lord." Lamentations 3:25-26

Hope is always a good thing, and it is even better when we hope in Christ.

Reading the headline of an article entitled, "How to Not Go Crazy the Week Before an Election" makes me realize that there is a lot of anxiety around us. At times, it is hard to wait. Those last days before a baby is born, watching the teacher pass out graded tests, or waiting for a phone call, we become apprehensive. It is just a part of life.

Recently, I needed to create a drain ditch to keep rain water from washing away the road. It seemed like a lot of work, so, as usual, I put if off. Then the ruts in the road became deeper, and I needed to do something.

A neighbor came by and said that it was not necessary to dig a ditch. He took a garden rake and dug out a shallow area away from the road. He said, "Now, the water will do the rest." And in a few weeks after the rains came, indeed, the water made its way creating a ditch big enough for the water to pass down the mountain.

It was such a small amount of leaves and dirt that were pushed away for the water to find another way to flow. The water needed some direction, and that small channel was enough. Much like life, we need to be careful that those little things we begin to worry about can lead to greater fears and worry.

Redirecting our thoughts to God and waiting as the Creator moves around us, we can find greater peace and joy. These are the days to focus on God's presence and God's desires for our lives. Sing a song, read aloud a Psalm, or simply be quiet and wait upon God. The salvation of the Lord has come.

The Obedient Plant

Therefore, to one who knows the right thing to do and does not do it, to him it is sin. James 4:17

Sitting in the living room looking out of the front door toward Lookout Mountain, I am always taken by the beauty of nature. Beginning with the pink obedient plants on the porch across to the view of God's glorious handiwork with the mountains. Hopefully, we all have that place where we can just sit and enjoy nature around us. We need a place to sit and be quiet to hear God.

Looking closer I see flowers being the flowers they were created to be, the trees growing as they should grow, and the birds busy singing and gathering their food. Nature just seems to know that the best way to live is to live as you are created.

And then comes these words: Then God said, "Let Us make man in Our image, according to Our likeness; and let them rule over the fish of the sea and over the birds of the sky and over the cattle and over all the earth, and over every creeping thing that creeps on the earth." There might have been a little undue optimism when God believed that we could do a better job taking care of nature than the Creator. We find it hard to keep the birdcage cleaned.

To fulfill God's purpose is not a difficult thing. We just make it difficult. It is somewhat of a miracle of how many ways we choose not to do what we should. Nature responds to crises in many ways, but then it settles back to doing what it was created to do. On the other hand we argue, go to war, and make up bizarre and ugly sentences on the internet. As the scripture says, we know to do right, and we will not.

There was a time at a church I served that we were going through a very difficult experience. There probably were ways for us to escape the coming disaster, but the church held true to its call to be people of "light." I asked one of the older members of the church what we should do. He simply said, "Do the right thing." We faced a lot of publicity, but doing the right thing allowed us to be a witness of God's grace and forgiveness. I received calls from community members that expressed their gratitude that the church did the right thing. The community knew we were not perfect and when we showed how to love and forgive, it was the best witness of all.

The "obedient" plant at the front door was planted to remind the grandchildren to be obedient. I think.

To Be Alive

He who forms the mountains, who creates the wind, and who reveals his thoughts to mankind, who turns dawn to darkness, and treads on the heights of the earth — the LORD God Almighty is his name. Amos 4:13

Get up early and go to the mountain and watch God make a morning. The dull gray will give way as God pushes the sun towards the horizon, and there will be tints and hues of every shade, which will blend into one perfect light as the full-orbed sun bursts into view. As the King of the day moves forth majestically, flooding the earth and every lowly vale, listen to the music of heaven's choir as it sings of the majesty of God and the glory of the morning."

- George MacDonald

I live half way up a North Georgia hill which probably would be counted a mountain in South Georgia. I can see Lookout Mountain and the ridges that lead up to it. Every day God paints a different scene in the morning at sunrise and in the evening at sun set. Angela says it is a beautiful landscape, but not as wonderful as a Florida sunset. Of course, Florida girls never forget the beach.

Every day, I think how God is so awesome, God is so wonderful, and God is so full of grace in my life. Like you, I am just so glad to be alive. But then I notice that I spend the rest of the day complaining about something. It is interesting how one can see a beautiful work of God, and then walk away totally forgetting the wonder of our life to fret about so much.

Our Creator provides for us a way to communicate with God. It is called prayer. And sometimes when we are too busy to pray, God will speak to us in a very small voice. Of course, now that my hearing is going, there might need to be some amplification of this voice. It is almost unimaginable that the Creator has such an interest in each of us and provides landscapes, prayer and even a nudges us at times. Our God who reveals his thoughts to mankind certainly must care for us.

My dog, Sadie, and I do not get to the top of the hill so much now. The heat, the hurting joints and nap times keep us from going. But sometimes we forget our fretting and climb up to the top. We can see more mountains and more beauty of God's hand. Sadie loves to chase a rabbit, and I am just so amazed at the wonder of God's work.

Oh, that I could hear the beauty of God's music all day long.

Persecution

Wait for the LORD; be strong,
and let your heart take courage;
wait for the LORD! Psalm 27:14

The Baptist Union of Ukraine sent out an update on what was going on in their nation. Of course, we can see through the lens of secular media the devastation and calamity of war. The devastation and calamity of war is in the report of the Baptist Union, but with the heart and emotion of those who believe in God and trust God through this critical time.

The Baptist Union reports of members of the churches that have been killed or taken into captivity. They speak of hunger and the mechanism for feeding and caring for people is almost non-existent, They report the large flow of refugees and the need for warm clothes and blankets. This is the result of war.

And then the Baptist Union shares stories of many believers praying together in the center of towns that have been destroyed by bombs. Members bring what food they have at home and share it in their churches with others. It is as if the loaves and fishes are multiplied in this time of need. The churches come together to worship and offer support to the communities that they serve. Amazingly, over one hundred billboards have been placed around the country with scripture written on them to encourage the nation. The Bible tells us to let our heart take courage.

Living and working in other countries, I have come across many Christians who have had to face persecution in their lifetime. In Peru, a family shared the courage of their family against the great Spanish Inquisition that sought to destroy Believers. There is an Inquisition Torture Museum in Lima that demonstrates what these Christians had to go through. These families spoke of the strength and faith they had in God during that time.

In the North Caucasus region of Russia, the few Believers that I met had to hide for many years their open worship service. They did not have a Bible in their own language, but faithfully memorized Scripture to share with others. And when some freedom came, they built churches to hold refugees and care for special needs children. They would take in any that no one else wanted.

On and on I could share the stories of people I have met along the way who have suffered and some who continue to suffer for their faith. And there is one word that I could use to describe their strong faith. This word is patience. "Wait for the LORD; be strong, and let your heart take courage." Christians who are under persecution have a strong capacity to stand strong and wait on God. They never give up and they never let the joy of their soul be taken.

And sometimes we find it hard to wait for the sermon to end. Has it already been 59 minutes? Can I go home now?

Rooms In The Church

Preach the Word; be prepared in season and out of season; correct, rebuke and encourage--with great patience and careful instruction.

For the time will come when men will not put up with sound doctrine. Instead, to suit their own desires, they will gather around them a great number of teachers to say what their itching ears want to hear.
2 Timothy 4: 2,3

One of the interesting books in my library is, "God Against Slavery And The Freedom And Duty Of The Pulpit To Rebuke It As A Sin Against God." It was written by George Cheever in 1857. I was struck by his call for the freedom of the pulpit and the duty of the pulpit.

"For the time will come when men will not put up with sound doctrine." These words reflect God's concern that there would come a time when people would not listen to sound teachings on faith. There would come a time when people would prefer conspiracies, sermons on how to be happy and just ignore the eternal plan of justice and love. "Their itching ears want to hear" that God agrees with them in their sin.

Growing up in a Baptist church I never once heard a sermon that slavery was bad nor that segregation was wrong. I did say once in a Sunday School class that I believed one day a Black family would be a member of the church. I thought we were going to have to call 911 because several people seemed to be passing out. I never was invited back to preach in my home church.

Studying the south and our strange dance with Christianity and sin, I found that most pastors who held the sacred pulpit on the Lord's Day preached freedom, but not for all people. They saw their duty to oblige the Christians to treat the slave with grace. It is unbelievable that it is hard to find one pastor in those years who would preach the Word in its season. Of course, there were pastors who preached against segregation. Their voices were drowned out by other pastors who did not.

In 1901, physician Leonard Gaston Broughton was called as Pastor to the Tabernacle Baptist Church in downtown Atlanta. He quickly observed "women of the street" who were sick with no place to go for health care. On Thanksgiving Day in that same year, Dr. Broughton opened the Tabernacle Infirmary with three beds. At the new Pastor's request, the Tabernacle church soon employed Georgia Barrett to do the missionary work among the "down-and-outs." When Dr. Broughton was asked how he planned to build a hospital, he responded, "With sick people and the command of Christ to heal the sick." In 1913, the Georgia Baptist Convention purchased the Infirmary and named it Georgia Baptist Hospital.

How many empty rooms do we have in our church buildings where we could share with those that are in need today. Walls of our church might be sending the wrong message of the hope of Jesus Christ when we find ways to exclude rather than include those precious creations of God in such need. But again the rooms in our church smell so nice and look so nice, why mess up a good thing?

Staying On Track

Now that we're on the right track, let's stay on it.
Philippians 3:16 (The Message Bible)

One of my new "pastimes" is tracking mail through the United States Postal Service. I have the deepest respect for my local mail person. It is laborious work to keep a pastor supplied with books all year. The issue of the route of a package shipping would challenge a physics professor. The problem is not created by the local mail system, but some upper management that has a desire to be a comedian.

I mailed a book in Chattanooga last week to a small town in Tennessee. It is not a long distance. It is about ninety miles away. So far, the book was in Memphis, TN for two days and now in Atlanta for two days. The last notice stated that "It is in transit and arriving late." I am not sure we are still teaching in school that "the shortest distance between two points is a straight line."

The Apostle Paul is reminding us that our citizenship is in Heaven. It is not to give up on the world in which we live, but to live lives of integrity. As the dictionary defines integrity as moral uprightness, we remember the teacher telling us to sit up at our desk. Our lives really are not our own but belong to God. We are the living church that stands on the solid principles of Scripture and moved by the Holy Spirit.

Yet, like a great locomotive traveling a set route, a minor fault of the steel rail can cause this powerful engine to violently derail and be destroyed. We have to be aware that to stay on track is to watch vigilantly the way that we walk. God promises to be a "light unto our path" so that we may not "sin against God."

Tango

Have I not commanded you? Be strong and courageous. Do not be frightened, and do not be dismayed, for the Lord your God is with you wherever you go." Joshua 1:9

A few months after the passing of Cordelia, our rescued Maine coon cat, I noticed a yellow tuxedo cat observing us from a rock on the hillside. She appeared to be assessing our capability of meeting her needs. Finally, one day she drifted down to our back porch where we had placed some food. After several days of taste testing our offerings, she decided to hang out with us.

Slowly she allowed me to pet her and then to hold her. She had deep scars on her back, her lip had been damaged, and her voice sounded like a pigeon. Evidently, she had been in a terrifying scuffle with some larger animal in the forest.

The grandkids named her Tango. She loves for them to pet her and enjoys my holding her in my arms. I can still feel the scars and see the damaged lip. Somehow, Tango made it through a very difficult time. Now, she has found her new home. Her task is to eat, sleep, and chase lizards. She welcomes all guests with a funny pigeon sound meow. She expects you to stop and pet her.

Her gentle response to life seems to be at odds with what must have been a scary experience. It causes me to think about how we respond to those challenging times in our lives. How can we keep those terrible things that have happened to us from affecting us in the future? Can our human spirit rebound from difficulty to pursue a life of joy?

In reading the Bible, it is very evident that God expects us to have stormy nights and days in the valley. The scriptures are filled with encouragement, warning, and promise that as these times come, God assures us that we will not be alone. Joshua has been given a big assignment to go forward and claim the land for God's purpose. It will not be an easy task.

The whirlwind that scatters our orderly life does cause us to rethink our priorities. Things that we had let lapse now become important: family, kindness, love. It might move us from the darkness of a life with worldly concerns to the light of God's forever still small voice of hope. And in the case of Tango, a life of bringing happiness to a bunch of children.

So Many Churches

And we know that the Son of God is come, and hath given us an understanding, that we may know him that is true, and we are in him that is true, even in his Son Jesus Christ. This is the true God, and eternal life. I John 5:20

Often, I am asked if Jesus is happy with all of the different Christian denominations and church groups? These types of questions are always an opportunity for me to think again about what we as Christians are to be doing today. Without any question, one can drive down almost any country road or city street and find a church building. So, is this maze of different understandings of faith a help or hindrance to God's design for His children?

In our country, we have been granted almost total freedom to start more churches that in turn often need a building. You probably live close to a church that is relatively new. And it probably does not look like the old red brick church of the past. This is on purpose. It might not even list on its sign what denomination it is, if any. This is also on purpose.

Yet, the question is, "Why so many churches?" There are as many answers as there are churches. But, "Is Christ happy with all these different churches?" As we know, we are all different. And when you drive up to your favorite fast-food stop, you can look around and there will be several other brands of fast food. In the current economy, we have the privilege of many choices for many things. This also includes churches.

Jesus was in a conversation with a lady who asked about this choice of place to worship. He said, "But a time is coming and has now come when the true worshipers will worship the Father in spirit and in truth, for the Father is seeking such as these to worship Him." (John 4:23). Jesus also said, "By this shall all men know that ye are my disciples, if ye have love one to another." (John 13:35). These texts give us a basic understanding that as long as you worship God in truth and spirit and love your brothers and sisters, God is pleased. No, God is not pleased when we see other Christians as the enemy or not keeping a particular covenant.

We should remember that Jesus gave His life for the sins of all people. God loves the world. There is only one body of Christ. And whosoever calls upon the name of Christ will be saved. And that is the truth.

Language

Have you not known? Have you not heard? The Lord is the everlasting God, the Creator of the ends of the earth. He does not faint or grow weary; his understanding is unsearchable. Isaiah 40:28

There must have been a moment of humor for God when I was created. God must have thought, "This child will go among the nations and not understand any of their languages." For most of my life, I have been around different languages. As a child, homes on either side of me were from other nations who had come to the local air force base to learn to pilot planes. There was a never-ending source of Greek, French, and German children for my play mates.

In high school, I finally passed French. In college there was Spanish. And then the absolute joy of learning Greek and Hebrew in seminary. "Passing" and "learning" might be somewhat extreme words to use. In my Florida pastorate, we started a Spanish church. In Ringgold, our mission to Russia entangled me with Russian and the two hundred other languages of the North Caucasus region.

Then to Japan for fun in Japanese. Later to Peru for more Spanish (both high and low Spanish). And then cap off my career in Lithuania. So, I return to my home state of Georgia. Being called to a wonderful and gracious congregation in Chattanooga, we invited a Spanish pastor to begin a church for the Spanish in the area. It is a marvelous group of Christians. But this past Sunday I was sitting with one of the Spanish pastors. He asked, "Bro. Bruce, do you speak Spanish? In a moment of total pride, I said "no." In fact, I do not speak English well (or good).

We mere humans tend to look at God through our own perspective. Our universe is constructed by our human thoughts. The expectations we have of God are designed from our own imagination. If we feel good, then God must feel good. If we feel bad, then God must feel bad. And if we do not have an answer, then God must not have an answer.

It is hard to move past our own language to understand the depth and height of God. "Have you not heard? The Lord is the everlasting God... " God is not the one to change. We are.

And probably, Saint Peter will say at those golden gates: "Feuch an cuir thu a-steach." (This was the language of my great grandmother) Oh, my, this is going to be an experience.

Spiritual Food

For I am the Lord your God who takes hold of your right hand and says to you, Do not fear; I will help you. Isaiah 41:13

From a Celtic Daily Prayer book come these words; "If I am truly poor I am dependent on others for everything, and I feel useless and worthless, and I realize deeply within that everything is a gift of God. Then with this attitude of complete dependence, I become useful again, for then I am empty of selfishness, and I am free to be God's instrument instead of my own. In poverty I begin to value everything rightly again. I see how little really matters, and I see that only that which glorifies God matters."*

I grew up on a small plot of land in southwest Georgia. My mother would often comment that if a Japanese farmer had this much land, that he would raise enough food for his family. Raking the leaves, I sometimes felt it was a large farm. But in reality, it was on one quarter of an acre. And I would often think about how it must be in Japan on such a little piece of ground.

One day, I was invited to a high school in Japan for farmers. The lead teacher, the sensei, showed me his quarter of an acre. It was used for teaching the students how to farm. It was a delightful day as we shared images of farming with American tractors that literally could not turn around in this small area. We talked about farming as an industry and a calling. He showed me bonsai trees that were over a hundred years old. As I left, he gave me a gift of a small Buddha sitting on a wood stand. My interpreter said, "that was his grandfather's and he wanted you to have it." It was that time of bonding over centuries over a quarter of an acre of ground.

We are just so dependent on God. God does not see us as beggars but as children that really need a lot of attention and many gifts. We are not only poor without God, the scriptures tell us: "For in him we live, and move, and have our being; as certain also of your own poets have said, For we are also his offspring. "(Acts 17:28) We are a ship with no harbour without God. We are absolutely dependent upon God.

We turn our attention to the coming of Christ. It is a time to release our hold on the world and to just let God speak to us. We enjoy our self-made ways, but we are spiritual people. The food we do without during this time is to make us aware of the spiritual. It is the spiritual food that sustains us and provides us with the encouragement and hope that we need. As soon as we finish our breakfast we think about what we should have for lunch. And then after lunch we think about what we should eat for supper. Oh my, bread is not our source of life, it is God's presence.

So, I hope we can let go and just enjoy holding the hand of God.

* Celtic Daily Prayer, Andy Raine, The Northhumbrian Community

Waiting

Yet the Lord longs to be gracious to you; therefore he will rise up to show you compassion. For the Lord is a God of justice. Blessed are all who wait for him! Isaiah 30:18

The cherry trees are one of the first trees to show their glory for the coming of spring. Soon, the dogwoods and then the wild azalea trees will reveal their amazing colors. The birds have already been singing as new life will quickly unfold for them. The sun, the soft winds, and just the joy of hope, all around us. The gray of the mountains begins to color itself again with the majestic beauty of a master painter.

We become somewhat impatient to plant something in the earth. It is our expression of faith that we have in the future. Experience has taught us that March sometimes holds a surprise for us with snow and freezing temperatures. The greenhouse is prepared for the seed and nature wonders where we have been all winter.

This is also a season that Christians look again at the unfurling of God's amazing love towards all people. It is our season of the spirit. This is a time of becoming less self-centered and more open to the birthing of the new. As nature often lays dormant through the winter, the spring sets all that appears dead to a new and vibrant life. Our spirit also needs that time of rest, but now we are awakened to the coming day of Resurrection.

Waiting is not a favorite pastime of anyone. We now have our cell phones to thumb through at the doctor's office or waiting for grandkids or a simply boring sermon. Even those times that are meant for us to be waiting for the Spirit, we want to escape. Even if the escape is into cyberspace.

Sometimes we are encouraged to give up something so that we are able to purposefully pray and wait. And then the church creates so many activities that distract us from this time of waiting for God to speak. God has much to say to us. But we need a welcoming spirit and open heart and mind. It is not a time to be filled with more religious things, but to listen and to hear and to know.

You and I know that we cannot do anything by ourselves. It has always been God who came through for us in our time of healing or hurt or sadness. Experience has taught us that when we wait upon God that He is faithful. And we are blessed when we wait for Him.

Homeless

"That the creation itself will be set free from its bondage to corruption and obtain the freedom of the glory of the children of God." Romans 8:21

The Christian writer, Thomas Merton, wrote "On the last day of January 1915, in the year of the Great War, and down in the shadow of some French mountains on the border of Spain, I came into the world. Free by nature, in the image of God. I was, nevertheless, a prisoner of my own violence and my own selfishness, in the image of the world that I was born." (The Seven Story Mountain) An honest Christian with an honest journey of wanting to know God more.

There is a homeless man that makes his residence around our church. He is not a drug user, nor does he drink. He just is in that place we are thankful we are not. The deacons work with him to keep his area clean and provide some direction in how to get into his own housing. But as yet, he is camped on the doorstep of the church. The city now wants him gone. They do not like his blue tent and several shopping carts filled with whatever. And so, what would Jesus do?

Our church has worked with the homeless for many years. They are far more patient and gracious than I am. The homeless man occasionally comes in for a prayer and sometimes leaves a dime for the offering. He is kind, but at that point we call the "bottom of the barrel." We want the government to take care of this issue, but they are at a loss of what to do. But you do know that God says all of life is sacred. The sheer numbers of the homeless in the future is unimaginable. Yet, it is our challenge to continue to see this man as the very image of God and not some homeless soul lost forever.

Thomas Merton really struggled with this issue of how God desires of us a holy life and the reality of living the holy life. The scripture speaks of "bondage to corruption." It is to be tied to destruction. We often tie ourselves to things that we know are not good for us. We excuse our human fragility for choices that we know will not serve us well. We are more in the image of our culture than our Creator. We choose not to see or to hear or to know that our calling is greater than what the world has to offer.

"The freedom of glory" is a gift that God seeks to give us. I have often noticed that people act differently around the church than in other places in the community. It is as if there are some unwritten set of rules we follow. Indeed, the church building is a nice place. But The Church is "us" wherever you and I might be found. There is not an exemption when we leave the church building. We can continue along the road that will destroy us. If the church is going to take seriously the needs of the souls that live around the community, that means you and I will have to do it.

I have been thinking, maybe if the man would get a camouflage tent he would not be so obvious. And just as a point, the city wants to charge us fifty dollars a day for his being on our property. Perhaps we could say that he is our watchman waiting for the coming of Christ.

Unselfish Love

"You that love the Lord, hate evil..." Psalm 97:10

The long shadow of Reverend Sam Jones has always been a part of my life. He was born one hundred years before my birth, and he became a lawyer and then one of America's great evangelists. With humor, wit and oratory, he captured American Christianity in the first part of the last century. The Grand Ole Opry in Nashville was built for his yearly revivals. It seems that our grandparents were greater sinners than we are since his preaching would be considered "Hell Fire and Damnation." You know, that was back in the old days when folks knew they were sinners.

He preached back in 1886, "I can tell who you are by what you hate and what you love." It is a reference to scripture that reminds us that God does hate sin, but God loves righteousness. In a very simple but basic way, he challenges us to see that our daily life is evidence of our faith. What are we loving in our lives? What do we hate in our lives?

Love Divine is the presence of God in our life. The old timers would laugh and sing, " I love everything, but I love myself the most." It is the challenge of every creature to desire the best for themselves and those that they love. It is the message of Christ that we desire that people see Jesus in us. And then, we want the best clothes, the best home, the best seat in church. We want our obituary to read of the glorious life we have lived. And then we meet our Master face to face. Where is the glory of God in our life?

I read this week that our wives might rather have their car washed than a box of chocolates for Valentine's Day. We so often mislead ourselves in what God wants in our relationship with our Creator. Love is perfectly unselfish. Paul reminded the Corinthians that love is not selfish. God does not count all of our wrong doing from keeping us from Him. God loves us not because we are good or bad. God loves us because He made us and wants us in a relationship with Him.

A box of candy is five bucks. A car wash is ten bucks. Ok big spender, what are you going to do?

Doubts

"Whether he is a sinner or not, I don't know. One thing I do know. I was blind but now I see!" John 9: 25

Marcus Borg, a Lutheran Christian academic, who taught most of his life at a state university in Oregon, shared his own experience of coming to know Christ. "Raised in the church, convinced Christianity was very important, committed to studying and teaching it, - even preaching it, respecting and loving it - I did not yet understand its central claims." In his book, *Jesus a New Vision*, he shares his spiritual journey of his unbelieving past to his believing present. For him, the birth of belief was a long journey.

There were those in the days of Jesus who thought that he was a religious fake. They traveled close to him to examine the results of his teachings and "miracles." They were simply trying to protect people from those "TV Healing Evangelists." In their examination, they summoned the man who had been blind. "Give glory to God by telling the truth," they said. "We know this man is a sinner." His response was simple, "I know now that I can see."

All of my ministry, I have worked in the world of "unbelief." And most of this "unbelief" was in the church. In Scotland, they talk about the weather because they do not want to talk about personal matters. In the church, we talk about budgets and programs because we do not want to talk about "our doubts." In Japan, it was easier to talk about faith to a Shinto/Buddhist than to Christians in the same country. Christianity is not easy. There are many very simple truths, but there are some challenging walks with Christ.

Hiking down a mountain trail, I just simply fell over on the path. It was a good path with no hindrances for the walk. But on this clear path, I just fell down. Back at the cabin I have a barrel full of hiking sticks. I missed Sadie, my hiking companion of years ago, because she would have shown me great sympathy. But there I was, laying on a good trail. How could this happen? My friend Joel Shore, a physics professor, would say it was just physics. My physician would say I should eat more vegetables. My neighbors would say a "lowlander" trying to live like a "highlander."

And we forget that our faith is not a recorded cell phone message. It is really a journey with "doubt." And when we understand that, we begin to understand faith. And sometimes we just have to get up out of our doubts and watch the beautiful mountain sunset and be on our spiritual journey.

A Different Prayer

"Be Still and know that I am God"
Psalm 46:10

Days on the mountain can be foggy, rainy, and cool. It would be a great day in Scotland. Tango, the cat, sits curled up on her chair sleeping. Occasionally, she will go outside and observe the squirrels that she should be chasing. I really think she is a pig dressed as a cat. But pigs cannot jump as high as she can. This is the time God has made for us to be still and know. But our cell phones insist that we should be going somewhere at this very moment.

The scripture of the Psalmist invites us to a calmness and the greatness of the presences of God. We think of the promise of a new year, but we can claim the promise of every day. We should take time to allow the birds to sing us a song, or the beauty of the clouds to draw us into a child-like search of the awesomeness of imagination. The Word of God has been passed down to us through the scriptures. Our Creator has made everything ready for us to come before Him and to know Him.

Grand children coming over is a joy in our life. We encourage them to tell us about their day. We laugh at their funny moments at school and have sympathy when something went so "amazingly wrong." We ask about their school grades and tennis game. They mark their growth on the kitchen door frame almost every time they arrive. It appears that their height is going upwards and ours is going downward. Such is the conversation God seeks with us. Being in the presence of God is about a conversation that shows us how much we are loved.

I enjoy prayer. God wakes me up at night to pray for a name that comes to my mind. It might be a family member, a friend, a former schoolmate or just about anyone. However, sometimes God says that there is something missing. I felt that God was saying for me to pray for someone I just did not like. Not just for a few prayers, but for the year. Of course, we pray for our enemies. But to pray for someone that I just do not like added a dilemma to my spiritual journey. So now I am praying for someone that I have never met but appears in the world press. It will take some time before my heart is set on this prayer. But, prayer can change things.

In the meantime, I read that eating pork rinds are good for you. Now I am on protein diet. I guess God said, "Bruce, you pray for those you do not like, and I will let you eat your favorite pork rinds." God is so good.

Time

"With the ancient is wisdom; and in length of days understanding." Job 12:12

Walter Moore wrote: "time is a great teacher and wisdom is not gained without it." Time is the one thing that is equal in all of humanity and nature. It is what we make of time that allows time to make us. Time can bring healing, working skills, and hope. It can also be wasted away by laziness and indifference. I believe that many people learned a new appreciation of time during the months of Covid restrictions.

It was not until 1883 that our nation had a standardized time. Until then, local communities would set their own time. There is still a cultural application of time by those who see life through nature or heavenly stars. Living in Japan and then living in Peru, I saw a different view of time. Vanessa Ogle wrote that "time as we understand it today developed from 1870 until 1950." I read that it takes 26 hours to change our time of 24 hours around the world.

You might have heard of the University professor walking across campus with a freshman. They passed a sun clock, and the freshman asked what it was. The professor responded, "It is a device that tells the time by the sun." The student responded, "Wow, what will they think of next?" However we might tell time, now is our time to live

A mountain preacher friend of mine tells of mountain time. On the mountains there are no square or rectangular fields to farm. Farming takes the shape of the hillside. Normally, the longer row of crops are on the top side of the mountain. The rows become shorter the further down the hill you farm. You normally start plowing on the long rows and slowly make your way to the shorter rows. My friend says, often an old-timer will say that he is "now plowing the short rows." Simply meaning, life is getting shorter for him.

Whatever row of life we might find ourselves, we still have time. It does take time to understand a lot of things in life. Serving as pastor of a church for twenty years and now in my thirteenth year at Ridgeview, I have seen the value of time in lives that I have served. I have found that the wisdom of a grandfather is often greater than when I was just a dad. I enjoy both, but time helps one see things differently.

The preacher Jeremiah said: "For I know the plans I have for you," declares the Lord, "plans for welfare and not for evil, to give you a future and a hope." Jeremiah 29:11

New Year

"But when the fullness of the time was come..."
Galatians 4:4

The New Year reminds us of the passing of time, and the hope of something good happening in the days ahead. We modern folks measure our time in digital minutes, cell phone notices and exercise repetitions. Distance is spoken in time and not in miles. We believe that time belongs to us. We are wanting to have more time to ourselves. In some ways, time is not seen as a gift of God, but a right to use as we choose.

Ancient folks did not have automobiles, internet or Big Boxes to shop. They lived with time in a different way. Time was measured in seasons. The season to plant, the season to rest, the season to harvest, and the season to give thanks. Time is a rhythm of the moon, the sun, ocean tides and the stars. Most of the world lives more with nature than with secular schedules. We get so upset when people are "not on our time."

In secular use of time, our Creator is often viewed as "waiting to the last minute" or "just in time" to meet our critical needs. We hold our cell phones as a scared amulet to defend against time. It is hard to carry on a conversation or an intimate moment without the fear of losing a call or scam text. Our heart beats so fast when time is getting away from us.

God is the master of time. "There is a time to be born and a time to die. A time to be happy and a time to be sad." God is above time, and observes time in the past, present and future. We will measure this year in hours, days and months. God measures our time in the eternal. Our time is precious to God,

75

and the greatest use of our time is to have time with the one who made us and loves us the most.

We become anxious about time. We worry about the days ahead. We see time almost as an enemy. Yet, the Creator of time desires only one thing of us: "to love God with all of our heart, mind and soul." When we feel that time is "getting away from us," is the very moment we need to stop time and be with God.

May the New Year give you time to really seek God and find what is your divine purpose. It will be more than worry or fear or anxiety. It will provide you with peace, hope, love and joy; just the things we have been hearing during Christmas.

Dreams

A righteous man regardeth the life of his beast (animals): but the tender mercies of the wicked are cruel. Proverbs 12:10

There is an amazing amount of Scripture that reflects on God's care for the nature around us. Nature seems to be a partner with God in carrying out the plan of the Creator. Nature is often mentioned along with the people in the promises of God.

In my growing up days, I lived in a wonderland of nature. In days past, kids were expected to stay outside of the house. Normally, our homes were not as large as we see today. And the sandy shoes were not welcomed on freshly mopped wooden floors. It was not a bad assignment to "Go outside."

My next-door neighbor had an alligator in his backyard. It was not so large. We had so much fun scaring the girls and the other boys from the other neighborhoods. One of the tasks that we had was to catch frogs to feed the alligator. As you can see, it gets to be more and more fun. My neighbor's name was Bruce like mine. He was a year younger, so I had the responsibility to give the orders as we searched for the frogs.

In one of his Boy Scout magazines there was an ad for the purchase of frogs. The company would pay twenty-five cents for a frog delivered to their company. Bruce and I did a fast calculation that we were on our road to riches. We built a pen with some water. We searched throughout the neighborhood and began to build up our astounding wealth. This was one of the best projects we could ever dream of.

After we had a pen full of frogs, Bruce wrote to the company telling of our great wealth in frogs. The company wrote back with good news. They would take every one of the "girl" frogs we could mail to them. The good news was met with some skepticism and head scratching. "How could you tell the difference between a "girl" frog and a "boy" frog? Remember, there was no Google back in the good ole days. It would be a couple of weeks before the mobile county library would arrive. We looked and looked over the frogs and could not figure out the "boys" from the "girl." And we sure were not going to ask our mothers and certainly not the girls.

Sadly, we opened the frog pen up and the frogs happily hopped off in search of better housing. We spent our last dime on popsicles. We sat on the back door steps of the house and had some deep philosophical conversations about nature. A few weeks later, Bruce brought me a horned toad from Texas. He said, "I think we can make some money from these toads." Well, the fortune never arrived, but we learned a lot about nature.

Sometimes our dreams fall apart. God will send us a new dream. And in the process we learn that God has some interesting things ahead for us. Maybe even a horned toad ranch.

Feliz Navidad

"And so it was, that, while they were there, the days were accomplished that she should be delivered."

The weeks before Christmas are traveling weeks for many around the world to visit their family homes. For parents with a car full of kids, this is a precarious time. It is a tradition to be around the family. Part of the journey is "not to sit on your brother's space" and continually ask your parents, "Can we stop now for ice cream?" And we hope to arrive a happy little family into the arms of waiting siblings and grandparents. Somewhere through the festivities we promise ourselves next year we might try Zoom.

Joseph and Mary made those hectic trips back to their families. The transportation was slower and much more dangerous. In this account, we read Mary was expecting her first child. Joseph was very aware the family might not be so welcoming. The Palestine greeting would be to share the best part of the home. But history has given us a hint that by being placed away from family there must have been some issues.

Indeed, the love of God for you and me was brought to us through the Son of God. This same Son of God who was at the beginning of our universe. "In the beginning was the Word, and the Word was with God, and the Word was God.' (John 1:1) God is the real center of this story. It was God who first loved us and sought that we should not perish but have eternal life. Jesus was the gift that acknowledged that God is so for us. God would send the Messiah. Even if the world was not waiting with open arms, God would present to us the greatest hope we could ever have.

Today, our world is much as it was in the day of the birth of The Christ. There are troubling issues around the world, families that do not receive their own with love and respect, and there's a lot of confusion about what the plan of God. Mary knew the plan of God. She said "My soul exalts the Lord, And my spirit has rejoiced in God my Savior. "For He has had regard for the humble state of His bondservant; For behold, from now on all generations will call me blessed." (Luke 1:46) Her simple trust in God carried her through some very difficult days. Could anyone on this earth love Jesus more than Mary?

We all clamor that we love Jesus. We sing of our love, we tell others of our love, and we express our love to Jesus in our prayers. But so often there is an absence of that love when we speak wrongly of others or fail to see the least that is among us or not believe when we really need to believe in Him. If we sing out, "Lord Jesus Come," may we be really, really be in love with Him

Feliz Navidad

A Mountain Monday

Jesus told them this parable: "Suppose one of you has a hundred sheep and loses one of them. Doesn't he leave the ninety-nine in the open country and go after the lost sheep until he finds it? And when he finds it, he joyfully puts it on his shoulders and goes home. Then he calls his friends and neighbors together and says, 'Rejoice with me; I have found my lost sheep. Luke 15: 3-16

In the day that I grew up, southern women knew their neighbors, they kept a new pair of stockings in their lingerie drawer, and they counted their sterling. As an observant southern boy, I was always amazed at how these wonderful ladies could keep their households in order with such few financial resources and the kids were kept in order with a small forsythia switch. Without Amazon or Google they provided for the family, and they knew everything you needed to know as a child.

The divine attribute of the southern lady was the ability to set a formal dining table with sterling silverware and good china; neither of which are in use today. But there was a day not too long ago, families would actually sit together at a table and talk to one another as they ate their meals. On certain special occasions, the lady of the house would go to the china cabinet and pull out the fine china and a box that held the sterling silver.

After the meal, the dishes were taken to the kitchen. The silverware would be counted and put away in the storage box. I never knew exactly why this was done. It was the final act of a formal dinner engagement. There have been many novels written where families divided over who should own the family silver. And some of this was not fiction writing, but the truth.

The Bible teaches the value of every person. Jesus uses the visual of the shepherd taking care of the sheep entrusted to him. It is much like today when every family member wants a stocking for Christmas and that can include the family cat or dog. Our hearts are a little more open to those around us during this time of the year. We believe everyone needs to be included. And it is this inclusion that brings a community or nation together. The best stories of Christmas are when the outsider is invited inside to celebrate.

God is counting more than the sterling silver. God is counting all of the creation formed in His image. Every soul has a great value even if we miss it. This time reminds us that God really, really would like all to be at the final banquet table in Heaven.

A New Hope

"May the God of hope fill you will all joy and peace as you trust him, so that you may overflow with hope by the power of the Holy Spirit." Romans 15:13

The writer Tony Gilroy spoke of his television series Andor on National Public Radio. The story is an evolution from Star Wars. He said that he has a large personal library on history covering several thousand years. He uses this library as a resource for his writing. In response to a question about how he begins a series, he simply said he would go back in history and study what already has happened. And then he made this remarkable statement. "I believe that I could take a dart and throw it into my books and wherever it landed I would read what is similar to our current situation."

The Christian community has long worshiped at the scene of the birth of Christ. And the scene has been recreated for a thousand years. The details of the event are not so important as the power of the story; God coming into our world and bringing a new hope. In every land and in every language there is a basic need for hope in the day we are living.

Christ is calling on us to look at our lives today. It is on this day that we need encouragement, understanding and wisdom. Just as in generations past, we find ourselves facing many of the same things that humans create. We feel the shaking of bombs in foreign lands, we weep for children that have been killed by guns in schools, and we wonder if we can economically hang on for the future.

I remember when I spoke to my mother as my children were looking at colleges to attend. "Mother," I said, "I just do not know how we can make it." Her kind response was, "We did not have the finances for the colleges you boys would attend. But God will take care of that." And yes, God did. It was a mother speaking out of history that she could bring hope for the future. It is this hope that Christians should gladly live and share.

"So that you may overflow with hope by the power of the Holy Spirit." These words remind us that the hope that we need is not a self-motivating hope, but a hope that God sets in motion within our lives. The Holy Spirit moves to bring the power of God into our lives to face the day-to-day life that we are called to live. Looking for the coming Messiah is about today seeing that hope of Christ that brings to us hope, peace, joy and love.

Thanksgiving

*In everything give thanks: for this is the will of God
in Christ Jesus concerning you.*
I Thessalonians 5:18

The beautiful autumn leaves have fallen and the coolness of the coming winter is slowly encroaching over the forest. The squirrels and chipmunks scurry around finding acorns and walnuts for their winter pantry. The birds that remain have hidden comfortably within trees and crannies of the outbuildings. It is quiet and almost desolate in the afternoons as you look out over the mountains.

The refrigerator is full of good food. Cabinets are loaded with cornmeal, cranberries and cream corn. I can see some cans hidden behind the black-eyed peas for the coming new year's day. The house is cleaned and a stern warning that my book collections will not be creeping up the stairs to show to family. "Bruce, they will not be interested in your new addition of a 16th century leather covered book."

Thanksgiving week is here. Family members have responded to their attendance. With the exception of a son-in-law that is sick and a brother-in- law that is patching up their Sanibel home, we will have a good crowd. The house is not large enough, but once we are all inside the warmth of the house fills our soul. We have so much for which to be thankful. Not only for one day, but for every day of our lives.

The Pilgrims arrived from England to escape the government's control over their practice of faith. They made a perilous journey to end their church's entanglement in the government. The church of England was a Christian church, but not the Christianity that the Pilgrims wanted to practice. And here we are today thinking it is a good thing to bring the state and church back together. Perhaps some are thinking the church will now be over the state. Oh my, the spider webs we weave.

Yet, in our minds during this week, the image of these Pilgrims giving thanks for their new opportunity strikes a strong cord in us. It is our heritage as a nation to say thanks for all of the blessings. We attempt to feed the hungry, we bring old blankets out to warm the homeless that are cold, and we sing "We gather together." In our human way we want everyone to be well fed, warm and happy on this Thanksgiving Day.

The scripture relates not to a time of well-being for all people, but of a time that is preparing for the coming Messiah. Words like darkness, drunkenness, thieves and wrath fill the chapter. It is an outline of how we are to be prepared by watchfulness, love, and living together with expectancy. This thankfulness is not about corn in the field or the pie on the table. It is about peace, supporting the weak among us and staying away from those who are evil. Thanksgiving is a way of living that shows faith in the oneness of our life with Christ.

Thanksgiving living is a greater joy than we might expect. It is a life of hope in God and even faith in others.

When?

Truly, I say to you, this generation will not pass away
until all these things take place. Matthew 24:34

The question from the beginning of humans walking on the earth has been, "How much longer?" Through the great flood of Noah, the escape from Egypt, the tragedy of Masada, the destruction of The Temple, the Disciples asking Jesus, and the recent political campaigns in the USA, the question remains, "How much longer?"

For those who believe this question is important, there are answers in abundance. Every generation from Adam and Eve until today accepted they were living in the final days of the earth. There is a long history of respectful and wonderful believers understanding that "this is the day" the Messiah will come. In the Christian community, we believe The Messiah, The Christ, will return.

I have had this conversation with the great saints of the churches that I have served. They had a strong understanding that they were living in the last day. They would speak of the scriptures that spoke about the weather, the political conditions, the sinfulness of people and other texts that proved the day was near. And here I sit, writing about this sixty years later. People get excited talking about the future.

The church I grew up in did not speak about The Tribulation. This is a time set of seven years when God will finish the eternal plan that was set at the beginning of the creation. In fact, the worry about the end of time did not become a part of my vocabulary for some years after I was ordained. I came along during a very prosperous time in America. People were talking only of a bright and joyful future. A young person would be able to get a college degree, a great job and live happily for a very long time. There really was no need to bother our enthusiasms with the idea of an ending.

It was not that I did not hear sermons or Sunday lesson on the Messiah's return, it was taught that "Jesus would return one day. We do not know when. So, work today for tomorrow and be prepared today for The Coming." And after fifty years of studying the Bible, that is where I still stand. Be prepared, but go to work tomorrow. In fact, Jesus spoke there would be people who would come to confuse, excite, lead astray those on this subject. Jesus did say: "But concerning that day and hour no one knows, not even the angels of heaven, nor the Son, but the Father only. Therefore you also must be ready, for the Son of Man is coming at an hour you do not expect. (Matthew 24)

And this morning my cat, Tango, did not get the memo on the Time Change. But she was ready when I came out of the door to feed her.

Vince Dooley

*"Where there is no guidance, a people falls,
but in an abundance of counselors there is safety."*
Proverbs 11:14

The former coach of the University of Georgia football team, Vince Dooley, passed away. He was greatly admired for his leadership at the University, and his passion for nature. As much as he was consulted for football, he was also consulted by gardeners throughout Georgia.

In high school, I played football for Newnan High School. The coach was Charles Harris who had been a famous running back for the University of Georgia. He was a gracious man, and a very committed Christian. Because of his connection to the University, he was able to invite the new head football coach, Vince Dooley, to our annual football banquet. It was in 1964, and this was Vince's first public speaking event.

Coach Dooley told a story of his coming to play football for Shug Jordan at Auburn. It was the custom for the football team to have a large steak dinner on Friday evenings. Dooley was the quarterback. He told the coach that he was Catholic and could not eat meat on Fridays. I imagine many of you remember having fish every Friday at school. Coach Jordan asked, "what can you eat?" Vince said he could have eggs. So eggs he did have.

The next day was the opening season for Auburn. In the game, Vince made some unbelievable plays running and passing. The team won by a large margin. Vince said after that game Coach Jordan made all of the team eat eggs on Fridays. And he continued by saying, "and you can imagine my popularity after eggs were exchanged for steaks."

This story was important to me as a high school senior. He was one of the many people God gave to me for good instructions. I was not a Catholic, and I could eat meat on Fridays. However, here was a young man of character saying that what he had learned as a youth was important. And if at all possible, he should do as we were taught.

We have all been under the influence of Godly folks who not only spoke of doing the right thing but lived it out in front of us. Today, almost everything that I read or hear, people are talking about being a Christian and the importance of the church. They speak with great fervency. However, as important as it is to talk about being a Christian, living it is more critical. As the old preacher said, "Don't tell me about your religion, show it to me."

Where are those who would live out for us lives of justice, peace, and graciousness? Where are those who not only shout from the housetops about the "One Nation Under God" but demonstrate love, hope and kindness? How can we speak about being for life, when we show such disrespect for others?

Perhaps, we need to quietly sit and eat our eggs and just show people what we believe.

Love

"Anyone who does not love does not know God, because God is love." I John 4:8

When I arrived in Japan, I discovered there was no Japanese word for 'Sin." Can you imagine what that would do to a Southern Baptist preacher? So, I must begin by demonstrating what sin is. No, that is really not what I meant. I must define sin so that it can be understood in the polite Japanese culture.

Yet, I am a man from the genteel south. From a young age we are taught not to speak openly of unpleasant subjects. If Van Brady had not taught us guys the facts of life in junior high shop class, we would have passed through high school with our high school senior ring still on our hand. But then, even the more serious issues of life were left behind closed doors so as not to trouble us. It simply was not polite to speak of unpleasant things.

And it was these issues of life that were left behind closed doors that have brought us to today. W.J. Cash was a journalist from North Carolina. He was educated at a Southern Baptist college and wrote the award winning "The Mind of the South." In this book, he sought to "understand the mind of the south." As another southerner explained, "Mr. Cash wrote with truthfulness and love." It did open the door to those unpleasant subjects we southern men needed to know.

What we genteel southern men did not want to know is all of the truth. We were taught in Sunday School to love our neighbor, give to the poor and send missionaries to Africa. We were not told of a history of fear, terror and death that had been a part of our history. It is not only from my neighborhood we were not told, but it was also from every neighborhood in the south we were not told. How can we speak of love when we have no idea of those we did not love?

The Baptist pastors of my day never spoke of issues left behind the genteel southern door. They believed for their economic wellbeing that we should leave certain subjects out of the pulpit. Of course, we listened about love, but in the context of the "proper" people to love. They spoke of respecting those who were our elders. But did not mention the poor among us. We wanted revival for the things that we believe in.

The scripture tells us that God is love. We celebrate that God loves the world. And so here we are in a divided nation, wanting the Gospel to tell us that we are the ones that God really loves. We shout at one another that "you are not a real Christian." We spend millions of dollars on cat food and politicians; neither of which will save us.

God loves the world, and God's children do the same.

The Boss

"And now, Israel, what does the Lord your God require of you, but to fear the Lord your God, to walk in all his ways, to love him, to serve the Lord your God with all your heart and with all your soul." Deuteronomy 10:12

The small daily appointment book that helps me keep my days organized listed Sunday as "Boss Appreciation Day." The little journal notes different days for several world religions, national holidays and the changes of the moon. It is printed as an all-inclusive daily planner. Receiving social security, I am allowed the right to keep writing on paper. You can keep your I-Phone, and I will keep my paper. Paper does not need to be recharged.

It was somewhat humorous when I saw "Boss Appreciation Day." Obviously, this was a thoughtful way to be reminded to say a word of thanks to the boss for our job. And being so reminded, I do thank God for my job. Once in Japan a Buddhist priest asked me who do I work for. He was fascinated that God would actually speak to someone. And it is an ongoing conversation with my eight-year-old grandson when he is at church. "Papa, who is your boss?" Evidently, I have not found the right answer to satisfy his mind.

In the Baptist church, we are "called" to be a pastor. This "calling" is based on our call from God to serve as a pastor. We are not "hired" or "employed" but "called" to serve the church. I have to pay one hundred per cent of my social security because even the Federal Government lists pastors as "self-employed."

This leads me back to the special day to celebrate our bosses. And I think we must all agree, I work for the best boss ever: job security because there is always a sinner lurking about, a great eternal pension with the promise of a fabulous banquet, and the boss is always present to give advice and encouragement. But then, the truth be told, you do get some strange, if not unusual assignments. Even with the assurance that the boss will always be with you, there are moments of fear and trembling. There are big fish in the sea, boats that sink and lion dens to be reviewed.

Yes, I am thankful for the days on this earth that God has allowed me to be a pastor. And what does God require? "... fear the Lord your God, to walk in all his ways, to love him, to serve the Lord your God with all your heart and with all your soul." It sounds simple enough, but it is not always easy. And sometimes when everything in the world seems to be at the most confusing or troubling, God reaches down, asks you to sit and be still. And then He reminds you, that He is really, really a great boss.

Andrea Crouch felt this need to say thank you; "How can I say thanks For all the things You've done for me? Things so undeserved Yet You gave to prove Your love to me The voices of a million angels Could not express my gratitude All that I am And ever hope to be I owe it all to Thee."

Darkness

*"He wrapped himself in darkness that covered him like a tent.
He was hidden by dark clouds heavy with water."*
Psalm 18:11

The bluebell bulbs arrived from Holland last week. In my absent mindedness, I had forgotten that I had ordered them. Neatly wrapped with two instructional booklets of forty pages, I looked at the bulbs with some apprehension. I am not a particularly good gardener. Perhaps, I had ordered these plants above my planting skills.

Instructions seemed simple enough. Dig a hole four inches deep and place the bulb in the hole. I cover it up with the rich mountain soil. Tango, the cat, looked curiously at me as I dug holes and placed something in them. Humans must seem complicated to the cat family. When the task done, I stepped back and said to Tango, "In the spring, we will have beautiful flowers on this hillside."

It is interesting that these bulbs will wait patiently in the darkness of the ground until nature calls them to come forth. The autumn leaves will fall, the snows will come and eventually the spring rains. The squirrels will play on top of them, the deer will step over them, and maybe Tango will check on them. It is one of her favorite place to sit where there is both shade and sun. They sit in the dark until nature calls them forth.

David writes a song about how God "wrapped himself in darkness" while planning the rescue of His King. We sometimes wonder where God is in the midst of crisis or tragedy. The "hiddenness" of God has always been a struggle for us. We see God in the sunrise, and in the birth of a child or in a moment of great spiritual enlightenment. But the darkness we enter at times is frightening and discouraging.

All Christians have experienced what David went through in looking for the salvation of God. We are in many ways like the bluebell bulbs waiting in the darkness of the earth to bloom forth in the daylight. David continues: "Out of the brightness before him, hail broke through the clouds with flashes of lightning. The Lord thundered from the sky; God Most High let his voice be heard."

God, the creator of life and of life around us, is still present. We might imagine that God is hidden, or we are in the darkness, but we are not alone. Jean Sibelius wrote:

> Be still my soul the Lord is on thy side
> Bear patiently the cross of grief or pain
> Leave to thy God to order and provide
> In every change He faithful will remain
> Be still my soul thy best, thy heavenly friend
> Through thorny ways leads to a joyful end.

God's Way

"And the effect of righteousness will be peace, and the result of righteousness, quietness and trust forever."
Isaiah 32:17

John D. Roth, The editor of *The Mennonite Quarterly Review* wrote:

Christians should embrace their political responsibilities not as citizens, or as representatives of political parties, or as a lobby group shouting to be heard, but as ambassadors of the Prince of Peace who came as a servant, welcomed children and foreigners into his circle, and taught us to love our enemies.

Somewhere along the way, we have misunderstood what the Bible means when it refers to the Messiah as being the Prince of Peace. One of the most troubling and disturbing places one can sit is in the midst of contemporary Christians. You do not know if you are at a political caucus, at a children's game being considered for the team, or a review of internet gossip. To sit with a Christian is to feel the peace of God and to know the quietness of the Spirit.

We are not doing the church a favor by all of the self-righteous malicious attacks we are eager to hear and quick to repeat. It appears we are judging others by our vocabulary of wanting a space just for us on earth. There is coming a place for us, but for now Jesus said, "My prayer is not that you take them out of the world but that you protect them from the evil one." The prince of peace is expecting you and me to be people of peace.

It has been my experience working with people that the ones who live a life of peace have a great inner peace. They do not get fearful or frustrated with all that is going on around them. They have a wonderful aptitude of seeing troubling times as a place to bring the peace of God. They make space in their life to meditate and to listen to God. The day will pass, and the night comes but they trust the way of the Lord.

We are selfish when we want it our way. Just a block away from my church in Tokyo was the Starbucks Coffee Shop. I would sit and watch as Americans would come into the shop and begin to order their coffee. On and on they would go about how they wanted their coffee. When they finished their very challenging order, the Japanese barista would point to the menu board and say, "Sorry, only these we fix." There were no options or "have it my way." The reactions of the customers was priceless. "You mean I cannot have it my way."

"And the effect of righteousness will be peace."

Yep, it ultimately will be done God's way.

Bare Feet

"My steps have held fast to Your paths.
My feet have not slipped." Psalm 17:5

I think that I have gone barefoot for a greater part of my life. As most southerners know, the shoes come off when you come to the door. Perhaps it is an old cultural trait that came from not bringing sand or dirt into the house. In those days, the old corn broom was the standard in keeping the floor clean.

In many countries across the world people do not wear shoes inside their home. In Japan, it was to keep the tatami mats clean. In Borneo, where you can find roads built of bamboo, bare feet was the norm. Even in Russia, there are spaces at the door to leave your shoes. So, it is not unusual in many places to see people being barefoot in their homes.

Once visiting the high mountains of the Andes, I came across villages where women never wore shoes. Even walking along rocky and rough trails, they would be barefoot. Some of the more popular dances in Peru were done with bare feet. Bali dancers always dance in their bare feet. The dance is a part of nature, and the bare feet bring that to a reality.

There was a church custodian who told me growing up in North Carolina that his family was so poor that he did not have shoes. When the snow was deep, his mother would allow him to wear her shoes. He said when he got close to the school, he would take them off and hide them. He had rather feel the freezing snow on his feet than to be embarrassed with women's shoes on his feet.

As we grow up, we might be missing a little joy by not going barefoot outside. Dirt on the feet might remind us of happier childhood days. In Asia, they believe standing with bare feet on grass or dirt will relax you and make you feel more at peace. I guess you could say it keeps us grounded.

Yet, bare feet also remind us of humility. I remember Christians from India would always take off their shoes when they came to receive communion. Jesus speaks often of our responsibility to wash the feet of the guest that comes into our home. The disciple Peter was surprised when Jesus prepared to wash his feet. Peter said, "Not just my feet but all of me."

Baptists in the South washed each other's feet in worship services up until about 1850. And then you know us Baptists. We will divide over most anything. So now we have foot washing Baptists and non-foot washing Baptists. But there are times we seem to miss the point entirely.

Well, washed feet or not, we should be careful "little feet" where we go. Dirty feet on the path to God is better than Nikes on the road to …..

Mountain Time

"For the LORD is a God of justice. Blessed are all who wait for him!" Isaiah 30:18

Longfellow wrote in *The Divine Tragedy* a poem of a conversation between an angel and the prophet Habakkuk. The angel spoke, "The tumultuous noise of the nations. Their wrath, their love, their hate." The prophet responds: "Surely the world awaits the coming of a Redeemer."

This is a time of waiting for God. The farmer has his "lay-by" time while he waits for the crop to ripen. The freshly made pie is "rested" after coming from the oven. This allows the ingredients to firmly set. There are those times we hear a statement that requires us to stop for a moment and to think about what was said. It is in the waiting that purpose begins to manifest itself.

God's people have had to wait many times in history. They had to wait in Egypt. Job had to wait. Jonah had to wait. They had to wait through the Holocaust. The waiting was not easy nor without questions. "Why" we ask. "How much longer" we cry. We observe the cruelty of man against man. We feel the pain of children who are undernourished or have no water to drink. We fear to question God, but we do anyway.

We do not like to wait. Stop signs on the road irritate us. The line is too long at the hamburger stand. We want to write an email to the postmaster about our slow mail. Yet, this time of waiting is not lost time to God. God is working out the eternal plan. God is not sleeping or seeking to bring us under duress.

God is first a God of doing what He says he is going to do. God sees eternity. We only see the moment.

I have learned on the mountain that folks will do what they say they will do. It will not be in city time, but in mountain time. I have a schedule, a long list of what needs to be done, and equipment that needs to be repaired. But I learned that on the mountain you have to wait until the potatoes are dug, Camp Meeting is over, and a new baby is celebrated. It takes some doing, but I finally begin to enjoy mountain time.

God has His time. And during this time of waiting, we work on our patience, our anxiety and our faith. We build our faith on the promises of God, we seek the justice of God within our community, and we feed the poor. The world continues with a tumultuous rage, but we, the people of God, wait for the coming of the Redeemer.

The City

*"But seek the welfare of the city where I have
sent you into exile, and pray to the Lord on its behalf,
for in its welfare you will find your welfare."* Jeremiah 29:7

The scriptures seem to move us from a garden to a city. About half of my ministry has been spent in the center of cities. Normally, these inner-city areas are struggling to hold on to some sense of community and wellbeing. I like both the country church and the city church. The challenges are different, but I am serving the same God.

The setting of the scripture provides for Jeremiah, who is an exile from troubles, a place where he could bring hope. And in doing so, he would be helping himself. We might understand that often people go to the city to make their fortune. Their welfare and prosperity is more important than that of the city. They become consumed by their self-interest.

Basically, God is saying, if you are concerned about the city's wellbeing, you will also find your welfare being met. This teaching is followed up throughout the Scriptures when we read of loving our neighbor, the golden rule, and give a man your coat.

Currently, God has led me to serve in the area of Brainerd in Chattanooga, Tennessee. The area of Brainerd was a part of the first missionary effort with the Cherokee Nation. The Brainerd Mission began in 1817, and our church sits on the original land. Later it developed into one of the more prestigious addresses of the city. The high school sits on one hundred acres. Every teenager in the 1960's and 70's within fifty miles would cruise Brainerd Road.

In time and cultural shifts in the area, it has found itself in a constant struggle. Some city officials want to rename it "Mid Town." As you know, we like to rename things so problems will go away. As many Baptist churches have discovered, it does not help. The area has a rising crime rate with gunshots coming down through our church ceiling. Homeless often camp around the church.

Most people in the United States now live in cities. And yet, Christians have escaped the cities to find comfort in neatly placed sub divisions. But what about our wellbeing? Could it possibly be that God is calling us back to the place we once prospered? Can we eventually see that the city is not where we go to get our share, but to share our life so others can also prosper.

Remember, we are all moving to an eternal city. So we could use this time on earth to help the cities filled with precious souls who are in need of God.

An Old Car

"For we have brought nothing into the world, so we cannot take anything out of it either." I Timothy 6:7

B ailey White is a wonderful author and radio commentator from Thomasville, Georgia. This is in Southwest Georgia where I grew up. It has some interesting and sometimes misunderstood peculiarities. In one of her books, <u>An Interesting Life,</u> she writes of the normal tendency for southern men to have an old undrivable car or truck in the backyard. In her case, her father had left his Porsche on the front porch of the house they lived in. Her father would say "One day we will drive that car to California."

For some this might seem strange. But for those who have such vehicles in their backyard, it is as normal as having banana sandwiches with mayonnaise or a paper bag full of hot boiled peanuts. And for those fortunate who have that old car or truck, there is a high dollar premium for those diamonds in the rough. People are driving through the countryside looking for these lost "antique gems."

In some way, I am making a case for my 1963 two door Plymouth Valiant with radio delete that now sits in my backyard. I bought it new in Bainbridge in 1963. When I went off to college, I left it for my mother who put 63,000 miles on it over thirty years. She had the same tires for twenty years. We brought it up to Ringgold in the last few years of her life. She told me that every time she stopped, someone would want to buy it.

It is the car that I took on my honeymoon over 50 years ago. And today, the grandchildren want to drive it. The problem is that it has no seat belts, a metal dashboard, and "iffy" brakes. For those who drove back in the 1960s, you understand "iffy" brakes. I do let them drive it when I am in a very good mood, but only for a short distance. They have their own cars, but they are always asking, "Papa, when can I drive your car?"

Now, I know I am not taking the car to Heaven. I imagine God is not interested in black tire marks on those golden streets. But it is hard to just get rid of it. The scripture about "take anything out of it either" has somehow not registered in my spiritual mind on this matter. It is just a car. Perhaps it might be a small thought, but maybe evidence that there are many greater issues that I have not let the Scripture control my spiritual mind and physical reaction. And that is one reason the Scriptures are so important. God is telling us the best way; the world is telling us an easy way.

And under my obituary there probably will be a notice. "1963 Valiant for Sale. Driven by a retired school teacher and an old Baptist pastor."

Faithful Sadie

He that is faithful in that which is least is faithful also in much:
Luke 15:10

S adie was our English Springer Spaniel that adopted us
several years ago. Unfortunately, she went totally blind. Her
character of being kind and friendly never changed. She
continued faithfully watching over our yard. Every morning
she walked out into the yard and follows the fence line to check
to see if there has been any invasion of her master's property.
As the evening comes and she is ready to go inside, she made
the same rounds to secure the property.

It amazed me that she continued her work in blindness. She
had a sense that she is responsible for certain things. And to
those things she was faithful. I would see her stumble around
rocks and trees. Sometimes she would get confused to which
way she should go, but never gave up. Blindness is not a reason
not to be faithful.

Indeed, I want to be faithful. I want to preach the great
sermons, lead thousands to Christ, and send millions of dollars
to world missions. But the reality is that God only calls me to
do what is needed of me. Be faithful, Bruce, in the day-to-day
work of faith. Speak with kindness to the one that wants to
argue about a certain political policy. Reach out to lift up the
one who has fallen because of sin without judging. Stand up
for justice when many sit in fear and silence. These small things
will not bring world peace, but peace where I live.

The creation has been around for many thousands of years.
Our basic human needs have not changed. Except today when

we are asked if we want to "supersize that order." Nations have come and gone, rivers have come and gone, and ideas have come and gone. Throughout these centuries God's plan has not changed. God's Word remains the same. We do not need to wait for the "next" edition of the Scriptures. All we need to do is to recognize that God desires faithful people to do as asked.

We probably will not be required to become super spiritual or jump tall mountains. What we will be asked to do relates to where we are today. What is God asking us to do to be faithful? We cannot feed the world, or protect all of the schools, or keep massive armies from invading other nations. But what about the fenced-in area of our life. Not just our family, but those who God places around our "God's Little Acre." There are so many needs, but there are a lot of Christians called to be faithful. Just be faithful.

Sadie amazed me as she stumbled around the fence. Our cat, Tango, watches. Sometimes she will run around the fence when Sadie leaves. Just think our witness of faithfulness might be just what the world needs to see. And maybe, others will join us to pursue the will of God for our world.

So Much Stuff

"Heaven and earth will pass away,
but my words will not pass away."
Matthew 24:35

One of my favorite seminary professors was Dr. Clyde T Francisco who taught the Old Testament. Every class was engaging as he spoke from years of experience as a pastor and as an academic person. One statement that he made in class shocked me. He said: "Look around you and everything that you see will one day no longer exist." This simple statement became a detour of my thoughts for the rest of the day.

There are so many things I enjoy around me. There is the beauty of nature, the magnificent architectural structures, and the friends that share a meal and conversations. How can this be, a world that passes away?

We have all invested too much into things. I am at that age where I should be aware of too much stuff. And sometimes I am asked what you are going to do with all of your stuff?" Maybe I secretly wish for the Messiah to come so I will not have to deal with it. We are the generation that have made a lot of things to enjoy. The environment will pay for some of it, but eventually, it will come back on us humans.

The scripture does astound. But one reality is that when we pass away, all passes away on the earthly level for us. There are also the sculptures that dramatize the last days of the coming Messiah. The theological question through the ages has been, "What happens to the earth?" God has created us for our environment, and it makes us wonder about what happen when our surroundings make such drastic changes.

God did create us to live. And sometimes our definition of living is not the same as God's. God speaks to us in words of peace, and love, and patience, and hope. We speak in terms of needing more, worried more, and engaged in habitual internet seeking. Perhaps our definition of living is not as good as our Creator. We do have a book of directions, The Bible. But we might also be the generation that throws the directions away as soon as our new toy comes out of the box.

God spoke at the very beginning about the creation being "good." Keeping a check on the work, there were times that God made things more pleasant for us. Now, we have a boy and girl and a garden. But then, our definition of how to live brings a great halt to that experience. And the next thing we know, we are out in the desert looking for water.

We are not people without hope. We are a people who do need to live first in the Word of God.

Catching Bass

"... if you do not listen to the words of my servants the prophets, whom I have sent to you again and again though you have not listened, then I will make this house like Shiloh ... "
Jeremiah 26:5

After a morning of moving the heavy pressure washer around the cabin and cleaning off several years of dirt from the logs, I went inside for a nap. My eight-year-old grandson said "Papa, let's go fishing." I explained to him that I was tired, and I had been working all morning. He said, "all you have been doing is watering the house." I guess it is perspective. An old man's desire for a nap and a young man's desire to catch a fish.

There is a growing difference in perspective about religious faith in our nation. The past few years has abounded in an exponential rise of groups identifying as religious. And not all things claiming to be religious are religious. As a pastor, I am intrigued by so many of these new groups beginning their name with "Christian" and ending it with some political ideology.

It is hard to be patient and to wait on God. We are not going to change God's time table or God's divine plan. It would be helpful if we would not take this time to worship false idols. We have always had a tendency to worship sticks, stones and clay and not our everlasting God. We build nations, institutions and armies to defend our perspective. Somewhere along the way, we might be missing the voice of God's prophets. "Some trust in chariots and some in horses, but we trust in the name of the Lord our God." Psalm 20:7

It is not fair to God to make the name "Christ" a name for division, anger, and hate. God loves the world, and that says a lot about the direction we should be going. God speaks of healing, of peace, and of justice. It might do us better to read the scriptures and get our perspective more in line with that of Gods'. But then it is as difficult to change as to be patient.

So, we grab our fishing rods and tackle box and head to the waiting bass. Walking along the wooded path to the pond, we begin to talk. It is a special moment to listen to a young mind and to find out what the world looks like to a kid. And it is a good time to be inspired to write an article. And yes, the bass were waiting for us.

One Nation

*"Now may the God of **patience** and comfort grant you to be like-minded toward one another, according to Christ Jesus, that you may with one mind and one mouth glorify the God and Father of our Lord Jesus Christ."* Romans 15:5-6

Living in Japan for several years I came to appreciate and marvel at how the nation sees itself as one. Their heart and work goes to the nation. It has been able to rise out the ashes of the atomic bomb to be one of the economic powers of the world. It is third in the world in Gross National Product. Their religious faith is both Shinto and Buddhist.

My Christian faith teaches and expects that we (the Christian church) be one. Not just in a confession of Jesus as Christ, but also like-minded to speak with one mouth. We are also taught by Jesus, "By this all people will know that you are my disciples, if you have love for one another"John13:35

The simplicity of the Scripture would leave one to believe, Christians are one and they love one another and others. Most Christians that I know have memorized this one scripture John 3:15. It begins, "For God so loved the world…" Before we let the theologians and Saturday night sermon writers do too much damage to the interpretation, the children would get it right the first time. "Papa, do you love Jesus? Do you love me? Do you love your neighbor?"

Our country proclaims that we are one nation. I believe that every generation has to define what being one nation means. Wikipedia says: "One" is an English language, gender-neutral, indefinite pronoun that means, roughly, "a person". For purposes of verb agreement it is a third-person singular pronoun, though it sometimes appears with first- or second-person reference. It is sometimes called an impersonal pronoun." Only in English can "a person" go to "impersonal" in one sentence.

Perhaps we have not clearly recognized what "one nation" means. When I think of "one nation" and what it means to me, the thought is clear. But when others begin to define "one nation" it probably will be very different from what I think. "One Nation" is a good idea, but we might need a few more years to really understand that term. It has taken Japan thousands of years to reach the practical practice of citizens truly being "One Nation."

And I give thanks to the kindness Japan gave to my family and to me in our years in Tokyo. Watashi no inori wa anata no tamedesu.

"God Bless America!"

"Listen to me, you who pursue righteousness, you who seek the Lord: look to the rock from which you were hewn, and to the quarry from which you were dug."
Isaiah 51:1

I have returned to the United States from most major cities of the world on Delta Airlines. It is said that southern men prefer Delta. There is just something overwhelming when you have been working in another country for some months to board that red, white and blue aircraft. It is welcoming, the crew speaks English, and even the restrooms are clean ... at first. I know I am going home when I take my seat. You just have that amazing "God Bless America" spirit when you settled down and know soon you will be back to where you were "Hewn."

Sunday's Prayer for our nation was led by Captain Haynes USAF, retired. His words resonated with me when he said, "God you have given to us different cultures, different ways to look at things, and different ideas. These are a gift to us as a nation. Help use to use these gifts for building your kingdom." What a wonderful spiritual perspective to see that those things that could divide us as a nation can actually help us to become a greater nation.

To pursue and to seek are active words. They demand work, sweat and tears to complete that which we are called to do. The great force of our nation is not in what we hold in our hand, but what is held in our heart. Our direction is not set by our desire to be great, but to show the righteousness of God. We are to be the "light" to the world. And as we sang as kids: "put it under a bushel? No!" Sometimes what we think is our greatest weakness can become our greatest strength. It is not by our might, but the power of the living God.

I think of my great grandmother Sloan who came to this country from Ireland. A strict Irish Catholic who never spoke the King's English. But her eyes would tell you what you might need to know. Settling into this new world she expected the children to work hard, be truthful and faithful to God. She saw this nation as a great hope for her family's future.

When I see the precious Guatemalans come to worship in our church building, I feel that same sense of hope and future. The girls with beautiful dresses and patent leather shoes, and the boys with nicely pressed shirts and ties. In time, they will adapt to our American way of dressing, but now, they want to thank God for being in America and sing praises in their language. On Monday, they will be working to install roofs on our homes and pick up trash on the Interstate. This nation is a gift to them. They are here to be "One Nation Under God."

Pastor

A good name is to be chosen rather than great riches,
and favor is better than silver or gold. Proverbs 22:1

What is the meaning of "pastor?" I am a Southern Baptist. It is not exactly an ailment or disease, but sometimes comes close. As the days have gone by, I have discovered that I am one of the "peculiar ones." I believe the Bible is the Word of God, I believe in missions, and Lottie Moon is a saint. Outside of that, I am often "suspect." I preach every Sunday, work to care for the congregation, and pray for our missionaries. But, I do not agree about a lot of shenanigans that have been going on in the Southern Baptist Convention.

A few years ago, The Southern Baptist Convention met in California. We have few churches in that state, but Baptists love to travel to "exotic" places. During this convention there came a time of making "resolutions." These resolutions mean absolutely nothing to the local church, but some preachers just like to hear themselves talk.

One of the big issues came to the surface about the word "pastor." I assume more Christian groups have the term somewhere in their vocabulary. But it appears that we Baptists have become confused about what the word means. In the previous year's meeting, a committee was appointed to study the word "pastor." The committee returned this year and said that it did not have a clear understanding of the word. It was determined that the committee should spend this year studying this word. One day we can find out what the word "pastor" means to the local church. However, we will not all agree on it. This is just a "Baptist" thing.

We have added so many adjectives to the word "pastor" that it has become confusing to our Baptist theology. We have the senior pastor, the executive pastor, the pastor of senior adults, pastor of children, pastor of youth, pastor of the gymnasium, pastor of worship, pastor of missions, pastor of ladies ministry, pastor of IT. On and on it goes. So now, we are not sure what the word "pastor" means. I think it is humorous, but my Baptist brethren do not.

The only time that I was called "pastor" was in Japan. When I began in the ministry, I was called "Brother Bruce." The church secretary calls me "preacher" (and bless her heart, she is from Sand Mountain). And yes, now she will put all of the salesman calls through to my office this week. When I am at the university I am referred to as "Doctor." That is always a scary thought that someone might have a heart attack on the Domain. But then they would need a "real" doctor.

I believe the result of all of this confusion is that a good name is to be chosen rather than a fancy religious title. The Spanish say, "Jesus es mi pastor." So, just call me Brother Bruce.

Summer As A Child

"Now learn this lesson from the fig tree: As soon as its twigs get tender and its leaves come out, you know that summer is near." Mark 13:28

There was a time in my life when summer was never ending. The best day of my childhood were the first day of summer. School was something of a past history, and now it was time to live a real life. This season was what I was created for. The endless hot days, the rain storms that would run you into the house for a nap and eating meals on the back porch. Fresh sweet corn, large red tomatoes, turnip greens served with sweet, iced tea. These were the days we knew nothing about calories and sugar content.

The first act of summer was a trip to the doctor's office to get the dreaded "bare foot" shot (tetanus shot). After that event, I celebrated with an ice cream cone at the drug store. Shoes will be only worn to church and birthday parties. From daylight to dawn there were the endless discoveries of nature, great army wars with the leftover tanks from WWII down the street and visiting neighborhood kids. Of course, the girls wanted to play "house," and the girls seemed to control everything. Even sometimes making us play the mother. The boys would get tired and go out on the dirt road to play football.

The times past are but memories of an almost idealistic life. There is such a contrast today with news we hear about our children trying to survive in a world they do not control, nor seemingly do the adults. The only concern I had about going to school was not being sent down to the principal's office for misbehavior, never touching a gun in the house or anybody's house and respecting all people. These were at one time the basic rules of life.

Now, we should be horrified at what our children will be dealing with. From sinful people it is hard to come up with a world that provides hope and peace and love. The struggle is not an answer, the struggle is wanting to live with the correct answer. And the bullies provoke wrath, and the profiteers buy the big cigars, and the drug dealers ride in the comical "tricked up" cars. And the least among us, the children, hear us talk about "and keeping you in our thoughts."

As the little boy was preaching to his backyard friends, he said: "God is watching us. Over and over he said that. Then one of his friends asked: "What else?" The preacher boy responded; "And God ain't happy."

Nope, "God ain't happy," and neither should we be. And believe me, when God settles this mess we're in, we probably won't be happy either.

"The harvest is past, the summer has ended, and we are not saved." Jeremiah 8:20

History

"Remember the days of old,
Consider the years of all generations.
Ask your father, and he will inform you,
Your elders, and they will tell you.
Deuteronomy 32:7

Kareem Abdul-Jabbar a former, a professional basketball player, was once asked if he did not play basketball what he would do. His response, "I would be a history teacher." He wrote that studying history is not an attempt to show ourselves superior to those in the past. History is about similarities so that we can feel gratitude and humility.

It is with gratitude and humility that I approach the pulpit each Sunday. I am incredibly aware that this is a sacred space for God's voice to be heard. It is also with the same gratitude and humility that I look out over the congregation. I see many members who are over ninety years of age. They have fought the World Wars, lived through the Great Depression and brought up their kids through the 1960's. They have kept the faith, stood for the justice of others, and worked hard their entire lives. I encourage them to stay off of ladders, don't speed on the interstate, and to just keep praying.

A great part of Biblical teaching is about the past. It is not only about the past of those who lived through those times, but it is also about our past. It is our family history. We read of great fishing stories, love stories, and miracles that modern people find hard to believe. It also tells of family struggles, battles lost, and clever people who attempt to trick God. The inspiration of the Bible is that it is about real people encountering real problems under the watchful eye of a loving God. Indeed, I should "remember the days of old, and consider the years of all generations."

An observation of mine is that we are not telling the stories of the past to our younger generation. We must contend with young ears filled with iPod and earbuds. We struggle with texting and are confused by those funny little emojis. But the story of our spiritual family is essential. It is for their well-being today and for their future. Maybe history is not our favorite subject, but it is a subject that we are a part of and have been created by.

God has been faithful in all. Throughout the Book of Psalms we read of God's work in all generations:

> *"Great is the Lord and most worthy of praise; his greatness no one can fathom. One generation commends your works to another; they tell of your mighty acts."* Psalm 145

Our generation has a spiritual work of continuing telling the history of God's faithfulness. We are all history teachers.

Deception

*"The heart is deceitful above all things
and beyond cure. Who can understand it?"*
Jeremiah 17:9

Rev. Henry Martyn, an Anglican missionary to India in the 18th century, translated the New Testament into Persian as he worked to build the Christian community in that nation. I recently came across a small track that he had written on deceitfulness. He writes about how we are so easily deceived by ourselves and others. And he writes of how we can even deceive ourselves about God. We might have certain views that we believe are God's but never realize that "God has ends in view that are totally disconnected from us." I am very aware of that as I study the scriptures.

Anyone who has internet connections or cell phones are constantly aware of people wanting to deceive us. There are calls for us to get great student loans for college, new warranties for our old trucks, and somewhere in Ghana there are loads of money waiting for us. Yet, it is not funny for those who have lost great amounts of their savings to fraud or been given wrong advice on health care or left love forlorned. The truth is that we all have been deceived at one point or another. Even with good education and the wisdom that comes with age, we are always a target. Jeremiah says: "The heart is deceitful above all things and beyond cure."

During our Covid-19 pandemic the phrase "herd immunity" was shared a lot. The World Health Organization defines this as "the indirect protection from an infectious disease that happens when a population is immune either through vaccination or immunity developed through previous infection." Somehow as the group comes to grips with the virus, more and more people are protected. I think that this same idea can be developed on how as a group we can have a "herd deception." As a people we have been deceived over racial issues, political issues, and even religious issues. And I believe the last one is critical in overcoming all of the other issues.

By our human nature, we will always be open to the deception of our heart. God knows our thoughts, and however pure and immaculate our lives may be, God will call us into judgement for the sin of our heart. We can pray to God to help us with deceits and yield our heart totally to Him. And when we earnestly seek God in this matter, we will find we have not always used our eyes to see or our ears to hear.

Holy Week

"It is a trustworthy statement, deserving full acceptance, that Christ Jesus came into the world to save sinners, among whom I am foremost of all." 1 Timothy 1:15

In the Christian community, there is a week referred to as Holy Week. It begins on Sunday called Palm Sunday and concludes a week later on Sunday morning called Easter Sunday. The intermediate week tells the story of Jesus Christ as He moves from a meal with His disciples to being resurrected from the dead. I mention this because many of the readers of this devotion are from different religious traditions. They are always gracious to listen and seek to understand the world of Christianity. For Christians, it is a very important part of our faith.

Holy Week is necessary because I have been a bad boy. It does not matter how bad I have been, I have not been good enough. I was raised in a very positive family where love and forgiveness was practiced with great generosity. In my mother's later years, her memory slipped on my behavior. Toward the end, she would tell my wife, "He was always such a good boy." To which she graciously agreed, but looked at me as she knew better. But in the grand plan of God's purpose for us to be faithful and serve our Creator's purpose, I come up very short.

I do try to be better. Yet, as Paul, the writer of today's scripture, to a younger Christian, says about his own life, "among whom I am foremost of all" a sinner. He understands that he has missed the mark about what God wants from his life. We can keep to all of the rules and be kind to pets, but we still miss the mark. I need not only forgiveness but hope that my life can be better.

I believe that Jesus the Christ came to help me. I do not understand why He had to come to die for my sins. But my New Testament states that He came to accept my badness so that I could live. It is an amazing part of history that God's son comes to care for my being bad.

Now, my life is to reflect that power of God and forgiveness in my life. My witness is to live to love my neighbor and to live in peace. These are the qualities that bring real hope to the world. My life is being changed. It is not in my power but in the power of God. The results of this changed life should make a difference in this world.

Holy Week is for bad boys and girls. And as Paul the Apostle to Jesus Christ says, "I am chief of all." It is a sad week for God, but at the conclusion, it becomes a week that sets me free to be a child of God.

Pharmacists

"Gracious words are a honeycomb,
sweet to the soul and healing to the bones."
Proverbs 16:24

Healing requires help from all of our being. We are made of spirit, body and soul. Each of these should be addressed when we are seeking wellness. Laughter, friendships, good medicine all go to mend our hurting body. Encouraging words, homemade chicken noodle soup or the prayer of a faithful believer can bring a new wholeness to our life.

One part of the professional medical field that I have always found helpful are the pharmacists. Growing up in a small Georgia town, the pharmacist played a critical role in community health care. Around the town square, there were several drug stores. These druggists were instrumental as the first response team to the daily illnesses or accidents that came our way. We would go to the physicians to get shots and have surgery, but to the druggist to care for almost everything else.

Druggists have seemed to me to be on the friendly side of the medical community. They have an endearing commitment to the community, and they give a genuine welcome when you show up to their counter. In my day, they were the healing philosophers. They dispensed medicine but also gave down-to-earth suggestions about what might really be your problem. They were a part of the city square. They were out among the people. You could walk off the street with no appointment and get help.

My life has been greatly enriched by pharmacists. They taped my big toe up when I almost cut it off with a lawn mower. Most of my scars were attended to by a pharmacist who did not fuss that I was hurt, but just asked how my family was doing. When I left for college, one pharmacist said, "Bruce, there can be a lot that can trouble you. But when you feel you are getting down, just get a coke and a cigarette and sit for a spell. Things will pass on by." It was advice I occasionally took.

Even today, when I am in a big box store or in a pharmacy, I walk by the pharmacist section. I still see the same smiles, the same concern as they talk to a customer. And if you give them some time they can give you advice to lift your spirits. They will work with you to cut the cost of medicines and alternatives to good health.

We should always thank them for their words of healing that they bring into our lives.

End Time

". . . and then the end will come."
Matthew 24:14

John Ringo is my son-in-love. He is married to my oldest daughter, Miriam. John is a military science fiction writer who has published over 50 novels and is often on the New York Best Sellers List. He originated the saying, "Get woke, go broke." Obviously, he is an excellent writer and storyteller. Should you be over a certain age, you probably have never read his books. He killed me off in one of his early books (You know the preacher had to go.), and I have been hesitant to read the ending of my life. He is good natured, and we enjoy a close family friendship.

Sadly, as the war continues in our world there is a lot of conversation about how the end will come to our world. Christians have a book in the Bible called "Revelation" and in the Greek called "The Apocalypse." This is one of the foundational works on the apocalypse. Those who have been raised in conservative Christian churches can quote "scripture and verse" on what will happen when the end comes. Although, there is plenty of debate about exactly how that will be. You know, two Baptists meet and have three opinions and one Gospel track.

There is a visual encounter that many young people are actively engaging in today with the dystopian and apocalyptic. It is a culture that conversation and ear plug listening brings to a new generation. Worrying about how things will come to an end is not necessarily the only thought of older folks. Each generation must develop and adjust to the possibility of a terrifying judgement and ending.. These I-phone games and

129

television series are written as fiction but believed as having substance to be close to the truth. My goodness, with so much fake news, what is true?

There comes a time of crisis at the climax of existence. We remember statements like: "Good times only last so long" or "We had better make hay while the sun shines." In a religious context, we are encouraged to "be ready" for the night that is coming. And in the secular community, there is an equal search for what the end will bring. There is an incredible art form of the apocalyptic in television, novels, paintings and music. We might be missing what this generation is asking.

The next time you see a car window with strange symbols, or kids dressed in black, or an unusual colorful poster on a wall that you really do not understand, you are looking at the statement "…and then the end will come." It is a different language, a different culture, and a different world view, but it is the same old question.

A Simple Message

His master replied, 'Well done, good and faithful servant! You have been faithful with a few things; I will put you in charge of many things. Enter into the joy of your master!' Matthew 25:23

The little New Testament that I hold in my hand was given to a Rev. Williams by his wife on August 5, 1969. It is well worn with almost every scripture marked as sermons and notes have been pasted throughout. There is a real presence of the sacredness of a Holy book. It was held in the hand of a preacher for many years as he proclaimed the Gospel. The book itself is only paper and leather, but the contents have brought life to many.

Rummaging through thrift stores is one of my favorite time wasters. I justify this obsession by looking for the history of our southern religious past. Christians in this area had few possessions. To find something that expressed their religious faith is important to me. Old pastors' Bibles are one of my favorite searches.. They are hard to find and frankly have little value in a secular world. But to me, they are a history of God's magnificent works.

Researching Brother Williams, I found that he had served several country churches in Tennessee and Georgia. He held long pastorates and was admired by the people he pastored through the years.. He did not go to college or seminary, but throughout his Bible you can feel the simplicity and power of God's word. And it is in that simple message that can be understood which transforms people.

Brother Williams did not preach Brother Williams, or some theologian or some other preacher. He preached from this small King James Bible the words that God gave to him every week. There is no building named for him, or book written of his life, or large financial estate left on this earth by him. But I am very confident that the words 'Well done, good and faithful servant!" were waiting for him.

So, what about us? Can we take the simple message of God's love for us and build a life of substance and faith? Can we hold in our hands the Word of God and be transformed into the image of the most Holy? Must we wait until Sunday to hear a word from God? Dare we seek God's voice in our life today?

Jesus told us: "It is written: 'Man shall not live on bread alone, but on every word that comes from the mouth of God.'" (Matthew 4:4)

Printed in the USA
CPSIA information can be obtained
at www.ICGtesting.com
LVHW041137310124
770460LV00064B/1421